Cost and Management Accounting

FIFTH EDITION

Cost and Management Accounting

AN INTRODUCTION

Students' Manual

Colin Drury

THOMSON

Australia • Canada • Mexico • Singapore • Spain • United Kingdom • United States

Cost and Management Accounting: An Introduction 5th Edition – Students' Manual

Copyright © 1987, 1990, 1994, 1999 and 2003 Colin Drury

The Thomson logo is a registered trademark used herein under licence.

For more information, contact Thomson Learning, High Holborn House, 50-51 Bedford Row, London WC1R 4LR or visit us on the World Wide Web at:
http://www.thomsonlearning.co.uk

British Library Cataloguing-in-Publication Data
A catalogue record for this book is available from the British Library

ISBN 1-86152-923-6

First edition 1987
Second edition 1990, reprinted 1993
Third edition 1994, reprinted 1995
All of the above published by Chapman & Hall
Fourth edition 1999 by International Thomson Business Press, reprinted 2002 by Thomson Learning.
All of the above published as *Costing: An Introduction – Student's Manual*
Fifth edition published 2003 by Thomson Learning
Reprinted 2003 by Thomson Learning

Typeset by Saxon Graphics Ltd, Derby
Printed in the UK by TJ International, Padstow, Cornwall

Contents

Preface

This manual is complementary to the main textbook *Cost and Management Accounting: An Introduction*. Throughout the main book I have kept the illustrations simple to enable the reader to understand the principles involved in designing and evaluating management and cost accounting systems. More complex problems are provided at the end of each chapter so that the student can pursue certain topics in more depth, and concentrate on the application of principles. The objective of this manual is to provide solutions to the problems which have an asterisk beside the question number and, where necessary, to supplement the main text with a discussion of the additional issues raised by the questions.

The solutions given in this manual are my own and not the approved solution of the professional body setting the problem. Where an essay question is asked and a full answer requires undue repetition of the book, either references are made to the appropriate sections of the main book, or an answer guide or outline is provided. You should note that there will be no 'ideal' answer to problems which are not strictly numerical. Answers are provided which, it is felt, would be generally acceptable in most contexts. Where possible the problems are arranged in ascending order of difficulty. A short description of each problem is given at the beginning of each chapter of this manual.

Finally I would like to thank, once again, the Institute of Chartered Accountants in England and Wales, the Chartered Association of Certified Accountants, the Chartered Institute of Cost and Management Accountants, the Association of Accounting Technicians, the Joint Matriculation Board and the Associated Examining board for permission to reproduce problems which have appeared in past examinations.

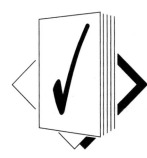

An introduction to cost terms and concepts

Solutions to Chapter 2 questions

Question 2.1

Answer – B

Question 2.2

See the description of cost behaviour in Chapter 2 for the answer to these questions. In particular, the answer should provide graphs for fixed costs, variable costs, semi-fixed costs and semi-variable costs.

Question 2.3

You will find the answer to this question in Chapter 2. Your answer should describe three of the items listed under the heading 'Cost objects' at the start of Chapter 2. A detailed description of each of the methods listed and the benefits of classifying the costs by the particular method is provided in the chapter.

Question 2.4

See Chapter 2 for the answer to this question.

Question 2.5

(a) See 'Function of management accounting' in Chapter 1 for the answer to this question. In particular your answer should stress that the cost accountant provides financial information for stock valuation purposes and also presents relevant information to management for decision-making and planning and cost control purposes. For example, the cost accountant provides information on the costs and revenues of alternative courses of action to assist management in selecting the course of action which will maximize future cash flows. By coordinating plans together in the form of budgets and comparing actual performance with plans the accountant can pinpoint those activities which are not proceeding according to plan.

(b) (i) Direct costs are those costs which can be traced to a cost objective. If the cost objective is a sales territory then *fixed* salaries of salesmen will be a direct cost. Therefore the statement is incorrect.

(ii) Whether a cost is controllable depends on the level of authority and time span being considered. For example, a departmental foreman may have no control over the number of supervisors employed in his department but this decision may be made by his superior. In the long term such costs are controllable.

(iii) This statement is correct. See 'Sunk costs' in Chapter 2 for an explanation of why this statement is correct.

Question 2.6 See Chapter 2 for the answer to this question.

Question 2.7 Cost information is required for the following purposes:

(a) costs for stock valuation and profit measurement;
(b) costs for decision-making;
(c) costs for planning and control.

For the alternative measures of cost that might be appropriate for each of the above purposes see Chapter 2.

Question 2.8 (i) See Chapter 2 for a definition of opportunity cost and sunk cost.

(ii) *Opportunity cost:* If scarce resources such as machine hours are required for a special contract then the cost of the contract should include the lost profit that would have been earned on the next best alternative. This should be recovered in the contract price.

Sunk cost: The original cost of equipment used for a contract is a sunk cost and should be ignored. The change in the resale value resulting from the use of the equipment represents the relevant cost of using the equipment.

(iii) The significance of opportunity cost is that relevant costs do not consist only of future cash outflows associated directly with a particular course of action. Imputed costs must also be included.

The significance of sunk costs is that past costs are not relevant for decision-making.

Question 2.9 See Chapter 2 for an explanation of the terms avoidable costs and unavoidable costs and Chapter 4 for an explanation of cost centres. A cost unit is a unit of product or service for which costs are ascertained. In a manufacturing organization a cost unit will be a unit of output produced wthin a cost centre. In a service organization, such as an educational establishment, a cost unit might be the cost per student.

Question 2.12 (a) A large proportion of non-manufacturing costs are of a discretionary nature. In respect of such costs, management has some significant range of discretion as to the amount it will budget for the particular activity in question. Examples of discretionary costs (sometimes called *managed* or *programmed costs*) include advertising, research and development, and training costs. There is no optimum relationship between inputs (as measured by the costs) and outputs (as measured by revenues or some other objective function) for these costs. Furthermore, they are not predetermined by some previous commitment. In effect, management can determine what quantity of service it wishes to purchase. For example, it can choose to spend small or large amounts on research and development or advertising. The great difficulty in controlling such costs is that there is no established method for determining the appropriate amount to be spent in particular periods.

For a description of fixed and variable costs see Chapter 2. Examples of fixed costs include depreciation of the factory building, supervisors' salaries and leasing charges. Examples of variable costs include direct materials, power and sales commissions.

(b) The £500 000 is a sunk cost and cannot be avoided. It is therefore not a relevant cost for decision-making purposes. The project should be continued because the incremented/relevant benefits exceed the incremental/relevant costs:

	(£000)
Incremental benefits	350
Incremental costs	200
Net incremental benefit	150

(c) An opportunity cost is a cost that measures the opportunity lost or sacrificed when the choice of one course of action requires that an alternative course of action be given up. The following are examples of opportunity costs:

(i) If scarce resources such as machine hours are required for a special contract then the opportunity cost represents the lost profit that would have been earned from the alternative use of the machine hours.

(ii) If an employee is paid £5 per hour and is charged out at £11 per hour for committed work then, if that employee is redirected to other work, the lost contribution of £6 per hour represents the opportunity cost of the employee's time.

The CIMA terminology defines a notional cost as: 'A hypothetical cost taken into account in a particular situation to represent a benefit enjoyed by an entity in respect of which no actual cost is incurred.' The following are examples of notional costs:

(i) interest on capital to represent the notional cost of using an asset rather than investing the capital elsewhere;

(ii) including rent as a cost for premises owned by the company so as to represent the lost rent income resulting from using the premises for business purposes.

Question 2.14

(a) (i) For an explanation of sunk and opportunity costs see Chapter 2. The down payment of £5000 represents a sunk cost. The lost profit from subletting the shop of £1600 p.a. ((£550 × 12) − £5000) is an example of an opportunity cost. Note that only the £5000 additional rental is included in the opportunity cost calculation. (The £5000 sunk cost is excluded from the calculation.)

(ii) The relevant information for running the shop is:

	(£)
Net sales	100 000
Costs (£87 000 − £5000 sunk cost)	82 000
	18 000
Less opportunity cost from subletting	1 600
Profit	16 400

The above indicates that £16 400 additional profits will be obtained from using the shop for the sale of clothing. It is assumed that Mrs Johnson will not suffer any other loss of income if she devotes half her time to running the shop.

(b) The CIMA terminology defines a notional cost as 'A hypothetical cost taken into account in a particular situation to represent a benefit enjoyed by an entity in respect of which no actual expense is incurred.' Examples of notional cost include:

(i) Interest on capital to represent the notional cost of using an asset rather than investing the capital elsewhere.

(ii) Including rent as a cost for premises owned by the company so as to represent the lost rent income resulting from using the premises for business purposes.

Question 2.15 (a) See Chapter 2 for a description of opportunity costs. Out of pocket cost can be viewed as being equivalent to incremental or relevant costs as described in Chapter 2.

(b) Depreciation is not a relevant cost since it will be the same for both alternatives. It is assumed that tyres and miscellaneous represent the additional costs incurred in travelling to work. The relevant costs are:

Using the car to travel to work:

		(£)
Petrol		128
Tyres and miscellaneous		52
		180
Contribution from passenger		120
Relevant cost		60

Using the train:

Relevant cost	£188

(c)

	(£000)	(£000)	(%)
Sales		2560.0	100
Direct materials	819.2		32
Direct wages	460.8		18
Variable production overhead	153.6		6
Variable administration/selling	76.8		3
Total variable cost		1510.4	59
Contribution		1049.6	41
Fixed production overhead[a]	768		30
Fixed administration/selling[b]	224		8.75
		992	
Profit		57.6	2.25

Notes
[a] $100/80 \times £2\,560\,000 \times 0.24$
[b] $100/80 \times £2\,560\,000 \times 0.07$

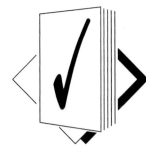

Accounting for labour and materials

Solutions to Chapter 3 questions

Question 3.3

(a) The managing director's conclusions are incorrect because:
  (i) Purchases may be in excess of materials used to produce goods for sale. In other words, raw material stocks may have increased.
  (ii) Material prices might have increased but the quantity of materials purchased or used remains unchanged.
  (iii) Stocks of WIP and finished goods may have increased, thus requiring more purchases.
  (iv) The actual selling price may have been lower than expected.

(b) Material losses may have occurred because of the following:
  (i) Purchase of inferior quality materials resulting in excessive wastage. This might be overcome by setting standards indicating the qualities required. If certain suppliers are known for the higher quality materials a list of such suppliers should be kept. Close cooperation is essential between the production departments and the purchasing department, and the reporting system should be designed so that the purchasing department is immediately informed when inferior quality materials are purchased so that steps can be taken to avoid this occurring again in the future.
  (ii) Use of inefficient and unskilled labour. This might be overcome by improving training.

(iii) Obsolete stocks. This can be reduced by setting maximum, minimum and reorder stock levels and regularly checking on the frequency of issues. A report on obsolete stocks should be prepared for management at frequent intervals, indicating the reasons for the obsolescence. All purchase requisitions should be initiated only by the storekeeper, who should check the stock levels prior to completing the purchase requisition.

Question 3.5 (a) (i)

Stores ledger card – FIFO method

Date	Receipts			Issues			Balance	
	Qty	Price (£)	Value (£)	Qty	Price (£)	Value (£)	Qty	Value (£)
1 April							40	400
4 April	140	11	1540				180	1940
10 April				40	10	400		
				50	11	550		
				90		950	90	990
12 April	60	12	720				150	1710
13 April				90	11	990		
				10	12	120		
				100		1110	50	600
16 April	200	10	2000				250	2600
21 April				50	12	600		
				20	10	200	180	1800
				70		800		
23 April				80	10	800	100	1000
26 April	50	12	600				150	1600
29 April				60	10	600	90	1000

(ii)

Stores ledger card – LIFO method

Date	Receipts			Issues			Balance	
	Qty	Price (£)	Value (£)	Qty	Price (£)	Value (£)	Qty	Value (£)
1 April							40	400
4 April	140	11	1540				180	1940
10 April				90	11	990	90	950
12 April	60	12	720				150	1670
13 April				60	12	720		
				40	11	440		
				100		1160	50	510
16 April	200	10	2000				250	2510
21 April				70	10	700	180	1810
23 April				80	10	800	100	1010
26 April	50	12	600				150	1610
				50	12	600		
29 April				10	10	100		
				60		700	90	910

(b) Cost of material used in April: LIFO – £4260; FIFO – £4350
(c) The weighted average method determines the issue price by dividing the total value by the number of units in stock. This will tend to smooth out price fluctuations and the closing stock valuation will fall between that resulting from the FIFO and LIFO methods. In times of rising prices the cost of sales figure will be higher than FIFO but lower than LIFO.

(a)

Date	Receipts Quantity	Price (£)	Value	Issues Quantity	Price (£)	Value	Balance Quantity	Price (£)	Value
Day 1							3040	0.765	2325.60
1	1400	0.780	1092				4440	0.770	3417.60
2				1700	0.770	1309	2740	0.770	2108.60
3	60	0.770	46.20				2800	0.770	2154.80
4				220	0.780	171.60	2580	0.769	1983.20
4	1630	0.778	1268.14				4210	0.772	3251.34
5				1250	0.772	965	2960	0.772	2286.34

(b)

Material X account

	£		£
Opening stock	2325.60	Work-in-progress	1309.00
Cost ledger control	1092.00	Cost ledger control	171.60
Work-in-progress	46.20	Work-in-progress	965.00
Cost ledger control	1268.14	Closing stock	2286.34
	4731.94		4731.94

(a) (i) Two of the following methods of pricing should be selected:

FIFO

Date	Receipts kg	£	Issues kg	£	Balance Number	£
1 Nov.					20 000	60 000
3 Nov.	5 000	20 000			25 000	80 000
10 Nov.	12 000	60 000			37 000	140 000
17 Nov.			20 000 at £3 = £60 000			
			4 000 at £4 = £16 000		13 000	64 000
20 Nov.	17 000	76 500			30 000	140 500
27 Nov.			1 000 at £4 = £4 000			
			12 000 at £5 = £60 000			
			7 000 at £4.50 = £31 500		10 000	45 000

LIFO

Date	Receipts kg	£	Issues kg	£	Balance Number	£
1 Nov.					20 000	60 000
3 Nov.	5 000	20 000			25 000	80 000
10 Nov.	12 000	60 000			37 000	140 000
17 Nov.			12 000 at £5 = £60 000			
			5 000 at £4 = £20 000			
			7 000 at £3 = £21 000		13 000	39 000
20 Nov.	17 000	76 500			30 000	115 500
27 Nov.			17 000 at £4.50 = £76 500			
			3 000 at £3 = £9 000		10 000	30 000

Averaged weighted cost

Date	Receipts kg	£	Issues kg	£	Balance Number	£
1 Nov.					20 000 at £3 =	60 000
3 Nov.	5 000	20 000			25 000 at £3.20 =	80 000
10 Nov.	12 000	60 000			37 000 at £3.78 =	140 000
17 Nov.			24 000 at £3.78 = 90 720		13 000 at £3.78 =	49 280
20 Nov.	17 000	76 500			30 000 at £4.19 =	125 780
27 Nov.			20 000 at £4.19 = 83 800		10 000 at £4.19 =	41 980

(ii) Job 124

	FIFO £	LIFO £	W/Average £
Direct material (Total issues)	171 500	186 500	174 520
Direct labour	50 000	50 000	50 000
Overhead	188 650	205 150	191 972
Total cost	410 150	441 650	416 492
Profit	45 572	49 072	46 400
Selling price	455 722	490 722	462 894

(iii) LIFO has produced a higher material cost and as a consequence a higher selling price to reflect the upward trend in material costs compared to FIFO. However, the valuation of stock under LIFO is a lot lower than FIFO as it is based upon older stock. Weighted average arrives at figures between the extremities of FIFO and LIFO but is not an actual cost. Note the effect on overhead of using direct material as a basis of recovery.

(b) (i) See the section on 'Treatment of stores losses' in Chapter 3 for an evaluation of continuous stocktaking. The advantages of continuous stocktaking are that:
(1) There is no need to stop production for stocktaking thus saving production costs.
(2) Discrepancies are highlighted earlier than with periodic stocktaking.

(ii) The advantages of centralized stores are as follows:
(1) Economies of scale (e.g. fewer staff and lower stocks).
(2) Better control and security of stocks.
(3) Duplication of stocks can he avoided.
However. if production centres are located a long way from the centralized stores there may be long delays in obtaining materials. It may also be costly in terms of transportation costs.

(c) (i) Economic order quantity

$$= \sqrt{\frac{2DO}{H}}$$

D = Annual demand
O = Cost of ordering/per order
H = Holding cost per item

$$= \sqrt{\frac{2 \times 400 \times 50 \times 150}{2}}$$

= 1732 kilos

(ii) Reorder level
= Maximum usage × maximum lead time
= 600 × 3 = 1800 units

(iii) Minimum level of stock
= Reorder level – average usage in average lead time
= 1800 – (2 × 400) = 1000 units

(iv) Maximum level of stock that should be held
= Reorder level + EOQ – minimum usage in minimum lead time
= 1800 + 1732 – (400 × 1) = 3132.

(a) (i) *FIFO:* Because the units contained in the closing stock are less than the most **Question 3.9**
recent purchase quantity, the value of the closing stock will be based on the
price per unit of the most recent purchase. Therefore the value of the closing
stock is £123.20, consisting of 44 units at £2.80 per unit.

(ii) *LIFO:*

	Receipts	Issues
Opening stock	35 at £2.00	
2.11.02		25 at £2
5.11.02	40 at £2.25	
10.11.02		38 at £2.25
13.11.02	30 at £2.50	
23.11.02	50 at £2.80	
24.11.02		48 at £2.80

From the above schedule we can see that the closing stock consists of the following purchases:

	£
Opening stock (10 at £2)	20.00
5 November purchase (2 at £2.25)	4.50
13 November purchase (30 at £2.50)	75.00
23 November purchase (2 at £2.80)	5.60
Closing stock	105.10

(b) The value of material issued on 24 November is £125.76 and is calculated as
follows:

	Receipts			Issues			Closing balance		
	Quantity	Price £	Value £	Quantity	Price £	Value £	Quantity	Price £	Value £
1.11.02	–	–	–	–	–	–	35	2.00	70.00
2.11.02	–	–	–	25	2.00	50.00	10	2.00	20.00
5.11.02	40	2.25	90	–	–	–	50	2.20	110.00
10.11.02	–	–	–	38	2.20	83.60	12	2.20	26.40
13.11.02	30	2.50	75	–	–	–	42	2.41	101.40
23.11.02	50	2.80	140	–	–	–	92	2.62	241.40
24.11.02	–	–	–	48	2.62	125.76	44	2.62	115.64

The cost of the 10 units issued to replace those previously damaged should be
charged (debited) to a scrap account and the stores ledger control account should
be reduced (credited). The issue cost represents abnormal scrap, which should not
be included in the stock valuation. Therefore cost of the scrap should be written
off as a period cost. If the scrap was considered to be a normal unavoidable cost
inherent in the production process then it would be reasonable to charge the cost
of the normal scrap to the job. For a discussion of the treatment of normal and
abnormal losses see Chapter 6.

(c) *Calculation of total hours worked:*

	Hours
Normal hours (£9600/£6 per hour)	1600
Overtime hours (£2880/£9 per hour)	320
	1920

Allocation of wages cost: £

	£
Capital expenditure (60 hours at £6)	360
Non-productive time (280 hours at £6)	1 680
Productive time (balance of £1580 hours (1920 – 340 at £6)	9 480
Overtime premium (320 hours at £3)	960
Shift premium	720
	13 200

The journal entries are as follows:

	Dr	Cr
Wages control account	13 200	
Cost ledger control account[a]		13 200
Work in progress account	9 480	
Capital equipment account	360	
Production overhead account (1680 + 960 + 720)	3 360	
Wages control account		13 200

Note:
[a]For an explanation of this account see the section on interlocking accounting in Chapter 5.

Question 3.12

(a)

(i)

	Y		Z	
	£		£	
Time-based earnings	154	(44 × £3.50)	180	(40 × £4.50)
Guaranteed minimum (80%)	123.20		144	
Piecework earnings	168	(480 × £0.35)	136.50	(390 ×£0.35)
Earnings	£168		£144	

(ii)

	Y		Z	
Time taken	44 hrs		40 hrs	
Time allowed	56 hrs	(480 × 7/60)	45.5 hrs	(390 ×7/60)
Time saved	12 hrs		5.5 hrs	
Bonus hours	9 hrs		4.125 hrs	
(75% of time saved)				
Hours paid	53 hrs		44.125 hrs	
Earnings	£185.50		£198.56	

(b) Time rate bases are preferable when:
  (i) quality is more important than quantity;
  (ii) employees have little control over their output.

Question 3.13

(a) For the answer to this question you should refer to the sections on categories of manufacturing cost in Chapter 2 and accounting treatment of various labour cost items in Chapter 3.

(b) *Current system:*

Total weekly wages	£960 (6 × £160)
Weekly wage per employee	£160 (£960/6 employees)
Average output per employee	1,000 units (6000 units/6)
Labour cost per unit of output	16p (£960/6000 units)

New system:

Average output per employee	1000 units (6600 units/6)
Weekly wage per employee	£180 (800 × 16p) + (200 × 17p) + (100 × 18p)
Total weekly wages	£1080 (£180 × 6)
Labour cost per unit of output	16.36p (£1080/6600 units)

Note that the above calculations are based on the assumption that each individual produces the average output of 1,100 units per week. If this is not the case then total wages will differ slightly from the above figure.

With time-based remuneration systems, workers are paid for the number of hours attended at the basic wage rate. An additional premium over the base rate is paid for overtime. The merits of time-based systems are that they are simple to administer and easy to understand. The weekly wage is known in advance and does not fluctuate with changes in output. Time rate systems have a number of disadvantages. In particular, there is no motivation to increase output, and this can result in a greater need for supervision. Time-based systems are most appropriate where the quality of the output is particularly important or where the workers have little influence over the volume of production.

With individual performance-based remuneration systems, wages paid are related to output. The merits of performance-based systems are that effort and efficiency are rewarded, and this generally results in higher wages, improved morale and the ability to attract efficient workers. In the above illustration, on average, each employee's wage increases by £20 per week (a 12.5% increase). The employer gains from increased production, higher sales revenue and a decrease in unit fixed costs. Labour cost per unit has increased in the above illustration, but it is likely that this will be compensated for by a lower fixed overhead cost per unit and additional sales revenue.

Individual performance-based remuneration systems suffer from the following disadvantages:

(i) Some workers may suffer a decline in wages. For example, a worker who produces 900 units per week would receive a weekly wage of £145 (800 × 16p plus 100 × 17p), a decline of £15 per week.

(ii) Performance-based systems are more complex and expensive to administer, and can result in complex negotiations and frequent disputes.

(iii) Quality of output might suffer.

(a) Labour turnover percentage

Question 3.14

$$\frac{\text{Number of employees leaving during the period (7)}}{\text{Average total number of employees for the period (42)}} \times 100$$

$$= 16.7\%$$

(b) Possible reasons for the labour turnover include:

(i) Promotion either within or outside the firm.

(ii) Personal circumstances such as moving from the area, retirement, pregnancy.

(iii) Dissatisfaction with pay or working conditions.

The costs of labour turnover include leaving, recruitment and training costs. Leaving costs include the costs associated with completing the appropriate documentation and lost production if the employees cannot be immediately replaced. Recruitment costs result from the advertising, selection and engagement of new staff. Training costs include costs associated with lost production when training is being given, defective work and low productivity during the training period.

Labour turnover and associated costs can be reduced by ensuring that;

(i) pay and working conditions are satisfactory and comparable with alternative employers;

(ii) adequate training is provided;

(iii) an appropriate career structure exists.

(c) The time allowed for 114 268 units is 5194 hours (114 268/22)

Efficiency ratio   = Time allowed (standard hours)/actual hours

                   = 5194 hours/4900 hours

                   = 106%

Therefore the labour rate is £4.738 per hour (£4.60 × 103/100)

Standard cost	= £23 892	(5194 hours at £4.60)
Actual cost	= £23 216	(4900 hours at £4.738)
Variance	= £676	Favourable

Question 3.15 (a) The accounting treatment of idle time and overtime are explained in the sections titled 'Labour cost accounting' and 'Accounting treatment of various labour cost items' in Chapter 3.

(b) (i) Wages paid (before share of group bonus):

	Direct personnel	Indirect personnel
Total hours	488	121
Normal hours	444 (12 × 37)	111 (3 × 37)
Overtime hours	44 (488 – 444)	10 (121 – 111)
Basic wages	£3 660 (488 × £7.50)	£726 (121 × £6)
Overtime premium	£110 (44 × £2.50)	£20 (20 × £2)
Total wages	£3 770	£746

(ii) Analysis of wages:

	Direct cost £	Indirect cost £
Direc workers:		
Basic wages	3240 (432 × £7.50)	420 (56 × £7.50)
Overtime premium		110
Indirect workers		746
Group bonus		520
	3240	1796

(iii)

Wages control account

Cost ledger control account	5036	Work in progress account	3240
		Production overhead account	1796
	5036		5036

(iv)

$$\text{Efficiency ratio} = \frac{\text{Expected hours for actual output}}{\text{Actual hours}} =$$

$$\frac{470}{(432 + 32)} \times 100 = 101.3\%$$

Question 3.17 (i) Re-order level = Maximum usage × Maximum lead time
= 95 × 18 = 1710
Answer = C

(ii) Maximum stock = Re-order level + Re-order quantity – Minimum usage during minimum lead time
= 1710 + 1750 – (50 × 12)
= 2860
Answer = B

Question 3.19 (a) (i) Continuous stocktaking refers to a situation where a sample of stores items are counted regularly on, say, a daily basis. Sufficient items should be checked each day so that during a year all items are checked at least once. The alternative system of stocktaking is a complete physical stockcount where all the stock items are counted at one point in time. Continuous stocktaking is preferable because production is not disrupted and any discrepancies and losses are revealed earlier.

(ii) A perpetual inventory system is a stock recording system whereby the balance is shown for a stock item after each receipt or issue. In a non-computerized system the records are maintained on bin cards or stores ledger cards. A separate record is maintained for each item of materials in stores. Therefore the stock balance for each stores item is available at any point in time.

(iii) For an explanation of ABC inventory analysis see 'Control of stocks through classification' in Chapter 3.

(b) For the answer to this question you should refer to Chapter 3 ('Relevant costs for quantitative models under conditions of certainty' and 'Determining the economic order quantity').

(c) Normal control levels are the reorder level, minimum level, and maximum level.

Reorder level = maximum usage × maximum lead time
= 800 kg × 14 days
= 11 200 kg

Minimum level = re-order level − average usage in average lead time
= 11 200 kg − (600 kg × 12 days)
= 4 000 kg

Maximum level = re-order level + EOQ − minimum usage in minimum lead time
= 11 200 kg + 12 000 kg − (400 kg × 10 days)
= 19 200 kg

Question 3.20

(a) (i)

$$EOQ = \sqrt{\left(\frac{2DO}{H}\right)}$$

where D = annual demand, O = ordering cost per order, H = holding cost per unit. Therefore:

$$EOQ = \sqrt{\left(\frac{2 \times 48\,000 \times £0.60}{10\% \times £10}\right)}$$

$$= 240$$

(ii) Number of orders required per year is:

$$\frac{\text{annual requirements}}{EOQ} = \frac{48\,000}{240} = 200 \text{ orders per year}$$

(iii) Total cost = holding costing + ordering cost

$$= \frac{240\,(£1)}{2} + \frac{48\,000\,(£0.60)}{240}$$

$$= £240$$

(b) Usage per day = 133.33 (48 000/360 days)
Number of days' usage in closing stock = 3 (400/133.33)
Lead time = 3 days
Therefore the next order should be placed immediately.

(c) Some problems when attempting to apply the EOQ formula are:

(i) Inventory is not always used at a constant rate, and the constant usage assumption is implicit in the EOQ formula.

(ii) The EOQ formula requires estimates of (a) annual sales, (b) ordering costs, (c) purchase price per unit and (d) cost of carrying inventories. These items may be extremely difficult to estimate in practice.

Question 3.22 (a) In Chapter 3 it was pointed out that stock holding costs consist of:
1. the opportunity cost of investment in stocks;
2. incremental insurance costs;
3. incremental warehouse and storage costs;
4. incremental material holding costs;
5. cost of obsolescence and deterioration in stocks.

Insurance costs can be controlled by obtaining alternative price quotations. The opportunity cost of the investment in stocks and obsolescence can be controlled by minimizing stocks. In addition, targets should be set for costs and physical quantities and actual performance monitored against the targets.

(b)

	Product A	Product B
Sales (units)	24 600	9 720
Add stock increase (units)	447	178
Production (net of rejects)	25 047	9 898
Gross production	25 300 (25 047/0.99)	10 100 (9 898/0.98)
Materials usage in kg (after wastage)	45 540 (25 300 × 1.8kg)	30 300 (10 100 × 3kg)
Materials usage in kg (before wastage)	47 937 (45 540/0.95)	34 045 (30 300/0.89)

Total material usage = 81 982kg (47 937 + 34 045)

Economic order quantity (EOQ) = $\sqrt{(2 \times 30 \times 81\,982)/(0.18 \times £3.50)}$ = 2 794kg

(c) Average stock investment (kg) = 2 794kg/2 + 1 000kg = 2 397kg
Average stock investment (£) = 2 397kg × £3.50 = £8 390
Annual stockholding costs = £8 390 × 0.18 = £1 510

Question 3.24 (a) (i) The cost of sales expressed as a percentage of total sales is 100 − Gross Margin %. Product A = 58% (100 − 42%), Product B = 54%, Product C = 63%.

Weekly cost of sales (£000s)

	Minimum		Maximum	
14/363	26 × 0.58	= 15.08	30 × 0.58	= 17.40
11/175	130 × 0.54	= 70.20	160 × 0.55	= 86.40
14/243	60 × 0.63	= 37.80	128 × 0.63	= 80.64

Weekly sales (units)

	Minimum		Maximum	
14/363	15.08/2.25	= 6 702	17.40/2.25	= 7 733
11/175	70.20/0.36	= 195 000	86.40/0.36	= 240 000
14/243	37.80/0.87	= 43 448	80.64/0.87	= 92 690

(ii) Re-order level = Maximum usage × maximum lead time
14/363 = 7 733 × 2 = 15 466 units
11/175 = 240 000 × 2 = 480 000 units
14/243 = 92 690 × 2 = 185 380 units

(iii) Maximum stock control level
= Re-order level + EOQ − (Minimum usage in minimum lead time)
14/363 = 15 466 + 25 000 − (6 702 × 2) = 27 062 units
11/175 = 480 000 + 500 000 − (195 000 × 2) = 590 000 units
14/243 = 185 380 + 250 000 − (43 448 × 2) = 348 484 units

(b) 1. Excessive stocks of item 14/363 are being held since stock exceeds the maximum stock level.
2. Stock is below the re-order level for item 11/175 and there are no outstanding orders. An order should have been raised.
3. The order for item 14/243 has been placed too early since stock exceeds the re-order level.

Cost assignment

Solutions to Chapter 4 questions

Question 4.1(i)   It is assumed that labour cost is to be used as the allocation base.
Total labour cost = £14 500 + £3500 + £24 600 = £42 600.
Overhead recovery rate = £126 000/£42 600 = £2.9578 per £1 of labour.
Overhead charged to Job CC20 = £24 600 × £2.9578 = £72 761.

Answer = C

Question 4.1(ii)

	(£)
Opening WIP	42 790
Direct labour	3 500
Overhead (£3500 × £2.9578)	10 352
	56 642
Selling price (£56 642/0.667)	84 921
or £56 642 divided by $\frac{2}{3}$ =	£84 963

Answer = C

closing WIP = Total cost of AA10 and CC20   **Question 4.1(iii)**

	Total (£)	AA10 (£)	CC20 (£)
Opening WIP		26 800	0
Materials in period		17 275	18 500
Labour in period		14 500	24 600
Overheads in period:			
2.9577465 × £14 500		42 887	
2.9577465 × £24 600			72 761
	217 323	101 462	115 861

Answer = D

Answer = D   **Question 4.2**

(i) Direct labour hour absorption rate =   **Question 4.3**

$$\frac{\text{Budgeted overheads (£691 125)}}{\text{Budgeted direct labour hours (48 500)}} = £14.25$$

Answer = B

(ii) Overheads charged to production = 49 775 hours × £14.25 = £709 294
Overheads incurred   = £746 625
Under-recovery of overheads   =   £37 331

Answer = C

(i) Budgeted machine hours = Budgeted overheads (£373 750)/Budgeted machine   **Question 4.4**
hour rate (£32.50) = 11 500

Answer = C

(ii) Overheads charged to production = 11 950 hours × £32.50 = £388 375
Overheads incurred   = £370 450
Over-recovery of overheads   =   £17 925

Answer = D

(a) Calculation of department overhead rates   **Question 4.10**

	Department P (£)	Department Q (£)	Department R (£)
Repairs and maintenance	42 000	10 000	10 000
Depreciation	17 000[a]	14 000	9 000
Consumable supplies	4 500[b]	2 700	1 800
Wage related costs	48 250	26 250	12 500
Indirect labour	45 000	27 000	18 000
Canteen/rest/smoke room	15 000[c]	9 000	6 000
Business rates and insurance	13 000[d]	10 400	2 600
	184 750	99 350	55 900
Direct labour hours	50 000	30 000	20 000
Overhead absorption rate	£3.70	£3.31	£3.00

Notes:
The calculations for Department P are:
[a]Depreciation = £170 000/£400 000 × £40 000.
[b]Consumable supplies = 50 000/100 000 × £9000.
[c]Canteen = 25/50 × £30 000.
[d]Business rates insurance = 5000/10 000 × £26 000.

(b) Job 976: Sample quotation

		(£)	(£)
Direct materials			800.00
Direct labour	P (30 × £7.72[a])	231.60	
	Q (10 × £7.00[b])	70.00	
	R (5 × £5.00[c])	25.00	326.60
Overhead absorbed	P (30 × £3.70)	111.00	
	Q (10 × £3.31)	33.10	
	R (5 × £3.00)	15.00	159.10
Production cost			1285.70
Selling, distribution and administration costs (20% × £1285.70)			257.14
Total cost			1542.84
Profit margin (20% of selling price)			385.71
Selling price (£1542.84 × 100/800)			1928.55

Notes:
[a]£386 000/50 000.
[b]£210 000/30 000.
[c]£100 000/20 000.

(c)

	(£)
Direct materials	800.00
Direct labour	326.60
Prime cost	1126.60
Overhead applied (125%)	1408.25
Total cost	2534.85

The auditor's system results in a higher cost for this quotation. However, other jobs will be overcosted with the previous system. The auditor's system will result in the reporting of more accurate job costs with some job costs being higher, and others being lower, than the present system. For a more detailed answer see the section on plant-wide (blanket overhead) rates in Chapter 4.

Question 4.11 (a)

		Departments				
	Total	A	B	C	X	Y
	(£)	(£)	(£)	(£)	(£)	(£)
Rent and rates[a]	12 800	6 000	3 600	1 200	1 200	800
Machine insurance[b]	6 000	3 000	1 250	1 000	500	250
Telephone charges[c]	3 200	1 500	900	300	300	200
Depreciation[b]	18 000	9 000	3 750	3 000	1 500	750
Supervisors' salaries[d]	24 000	12 800	7 200	4 000		
Heat and light[a]	6 400	3 000	1 800	600	600	400
	70 400					
Allocated		2 800	1 700	1 200	800	600
		38 100	20 200	11 300	4 900	3 000
Reapportionment of X		2 450 (50%)	1 225 (25%)	1 225 (25%)	(4 900)	
Reapportionment of Y		600 (20%)	900 (30%)	1 500 (50%)		(3 000)
		£41 150	£22 325	£14 025		
Budgeted D.L. hours[e]		3 200	1 800	1 000		
Absorption rates		£12.86	£12.40	£14.02		

Notes
[a]Apportioned on the basis of floor area.
[b]Apportioned on the basis of machine value.

^cShould be apportioned on the basis of the number of telephone points or estimated usage. This information is not given and an alternative arbitrary method of apportionment should be chosen. In the above analysis telephone charges have been apportioned on the basis of floor area.

^dApportioned on the basis of direct labour hours.

^eMachine hours are not given but direct labour hours are. It is assumed that the examiner requires absorption to be on the basis of direct labour hours.

(b)

		Job 123	Job 124
		(£)	(£)
Direct material		154.00	108.00
Direct labour:			
	Department A	76.00	60.80
	Department B	42.00	35.00
	Department C	34.00	47.60
Total direct cost		306.00	251.40
Overhead:			
	Department A	257.20	205.76
	Department B	148.80	124.00
	Department C	140.20	196.28
Total cost		852.20	777.44
Profit		284.07	259.15
(c)	Listed selling price	1136.27	1036.59

Note

Let SP represent selling price.

Cost + 0.25SP = SP

Job 123: £852.20 + 0.25SP = 1SP

0.75SP = £852.20

Hence SP = £1136.27

For Job 124: 0.75SP = £777.44

Hence SP = £1036.59

(d) For the answer to this question see sections on materials recording procedure and pricing the issues of materials in Chapter 3.

Question 4.13

(a)

Calculation of overhead absorption rates

	Machining (£000)	Assembly (£000)	Finishing (£000)	Stores (£000)	Maintenance (£000)
Allocated costs	600.00	250.00	150.00	100.00	80.00
Stores apportionment	40.00 (40%)	30.00 (30%)	20.00 (20%)	(100.00)	10.00 (10%)
Maintenance apportionment	49.50 (55%)	18.00 (20%)	18.00 (20%)	4.50 (5%)	(90.00)
Stores apportionment^a	2.00 (4/9)	1.50 (3/9)	1.00 (2/9)	(4.50)	
Total	691.50	299.50	189.00	—	—
Machine hours	50 000				
Labour hours		30 000	20 000		
Overhead absorption rates^b	13.83	9.98	9.45		

Notes

^a Costs have become too small at this stage to justify apportioning 10% of the costs to the maintenance department. Therefore stores costs are apportioned in the ratio 40: 30: 20.

^b Machine hours are the predominant activity in the machine department whereas labour hours are the predominant activity in the assembly and finishing departments. Therefore machine hours are used as the allocation base in the machining department and direct labour hours are used for the assembly and finishing departments.

(b)

Quotation for job XX 34

	(£)	(£)
Direct material		2400.00
Direct labour		1500.00
Overhead cost:		
Machining (45 machine hours at £13.83)	622.35	
Assembly (15 labour hours at £9.98)	149.70	
Finishing (12 labour hours at £9.45	113.40	885.45
Total cost		4785.45

Selling price (Profit margin = 20% of selling price
∴ selling price = £4785.45/0.8)   5981.81

(c)

Overhead control account

	(£)		(£)
Overhead incurred	300 000	WIP control (30 700 hrs at £9.98)	306 386
Balance – over-recovery transferred to costing profit and loss account	6 386		
	306 386		306 386

(d) For the answer to this question see 'An illustration of the two-stage process for an ABC system' in Chapter 11. In particular, the answer should stress that cost centres will consist of activity cost centres rather than departmental centres. Separate cost driver rates would also be established for the service departments and the costs would be allocated to cost objects via cost driver rates rather than being reallocated to production departments and assigned within the production department rates. The answer should also stress that instead of using just two volume-based cost drivers (e.g. direct labour and machine hours) a variety of cost drivers would be used, including non-volume-based drivers such as number of set-ups and number of material issues. The answer could also stress that within the machining department a separate set-up activity centre might be established with costs being assigned using the number of set-ups as the cost driver. The current system includes the set-up costs within the machine hour overhead rate.

Question 4.14 (a)

	(£)	(£)
Photography: 64 pages at £150 per page		9 600
Set-up:		
Labour – 64 plates × 4 hours per plate = 256 hours at £7 per hour	1 792	
Materials – 64 plates at £35 per plate	2 240	
Overhead – 256 labour hours at £9.50 per hour	2 432	
		6 464

Printing:

Materials (paper):
$$100\,000 \text{ catalogues} \times 32 \text{ sheets} \times \frac{£12}{1000} \times \frac{100}{98}$$ 39 184

Materials (other):
$$\frac{100\,000}{500} \times £7$$ 1 400

Labour and Overheads
$$\frac{100\,000}{1000} \text{ m/c hours at £62 per hour}$$ 6 200

    46 784

Binding:
    Labour and Overheads

$$\frac{100\,000}{2500} \text{ m/c hours at £43 per hour} \qquad\qquad\qquad 1\,720$$

    Total costs   64 568

$$\text{Selling price} - £64\,568 \times \frac{100}{90} \qquad\qquad\qquad 71\,742$$

(b) Estimated hours = 256

$$\text{Actual hours} = 256 \times \frac{100}{90}$$
$$= 284.4$$

Additional costs = (284.4 − 256) × £16.50 (£7 labour rate + £9.50 overhead rate)
                   = £469.3

(i)   Percentage of direct material cost $= \dfrac{£250\,000}{£100\,000} \times 100 = 250\%$

     Direct labour hour rate   = £250 000/50 000 hours = £5 per hour

(ii) Percentage material cost   = 250% × £7000 = £17 500

     Direct labour cost   = 800 × £5 = £4000

(iii) Overhead incurred £350 000

     Overhead absorbed £275 000 (55 000 × £5)

     Under absorption of overhead £75 000

     The under absorption of overhead should be regarded as a period cost and charged to the profit and loss account.

(iv) The answer should stress the limitations of the percentage of direct material cost method and justify why the direct labour hour method is the most frequently used method in non-machine paced environments. See Appendix 4.2 for a more detailed answer to this question.

(a)

	Department A	Department B
Allocated costs	£217 860	£374 450
Apportioned costs	45 150	58 820
Total departmental overheads	263 010	433 270
Overhead absorption rate	£19.16 (£263 010/13 730)	£26.89 (£433 270/16 110)

(b)

	Department A (£)	Department B (£)	Department C (£)
Allocated costs	219 917	387 181	103 254
Apportionment of 70% of Department C costs [a]	32 267	40 011	(72 278)
Apportionment of 30% of Department C costs [b]	11 555	19 421	(30 976)
Total departmental overheads	263 739	446 613	
Overheads charged to production	261 956 [c]	455 866 [d]	
Under/(over-recovery)	1 783	(9 253)	

Notes:

[a] Allocated on the basis of actual machine hours

[b] Allocated on the basis of actual direct labour hours

[c] £19.16 × 13 672 actual machine hours

[d] £26.89 × 16 953 actual direct labour hours

(c)

    See Appendix 4.1 (Chapter 4) for the answer to this question.

Question 4.19 (a) *Year 1*

(1)	Budgeted machine hours	132 500
(2)	Budgeted fixed overheads	£2 411 500 (132 500 × £18.20)
(3)	Actual machine hours	134 200 (£2 442 440/£18.20)
(4)	Fixed overheads absorbed	£2 442 440
(5)	Actual fixed overheads incurred	£2 317 461
	Over-absorption of fixed overheads	£124 979 (5 − 4)

The section on 'Under- and over-recovery of fixed overheads' in Chapter 4 indicates that an under- or over-recovery will arise whenever actual activity or expenditure differs from budgeted activity or expenditure. Actual activity was 1700 hours in excess of budget and this will result in an over-recovery of fixed overheads of £30 940. Actual overheads incurred were £94 039 (£2 317 461 – £2 411 500) less than budget and this is the second factor explaining the over-absorption of fixed overheads.

Summary	(£)
Over-recovery due to actual expenditure being less than budgeted expenditure	94 039
Over-recovery due to actual activity exceeding budgeted activity	30 940
Total over-recovery of overhead for year 1	124 979

Year 2

(1)	Budgeted machine hours (134 200 × 1.05)	140 910
(2)	Budgeted fixed overheads	£2 620 926
(3)	Fixed overhead rate (£2 620 926/140 900 hours)	£18.60
(4)	Actual fixed overheads incurred	£2 695 721
(5)	Fixed overheads absorbed (139 260 × £18.60)	£2 590 236
(6)	Under-recovery of overhead for year 2 (4 – 5)	£105 485

Analysis of under-recovery of overhead	(£)
Under-recovery due to actual activity being less than budgeted activity (139 260 – 140 910) × £18.60	30 690
Under-recovery due to actual expenditure being greater than budgeted expenditure (£2 695 721 − £2 620 926	74 795
Total under-recovery for the year	105 485

Change in the overhead rate

Change in the rate (£18.60 – £18.20)/£18.20	=	+ 2.198%
This can be analysed as follows:		
Increase in budgeted expenditure (£2 620 926 – £2 411 500)/£2 411 500	=	+ 8.684%
Increase in budgeted activity (140 910 hours – 132 500 hrs)/132 500	=	+ 6.347%

The increase of 2.198% in the absorption rate is due to an expenditure increase of 8.684% in budgeted expenditure partly offset by an increase in budgeted activity of 6.347% over the 2 years.

Proof
(1.08684/1.06347) − 1 = 0.02198 (2.198%)

(b) See 'Plant-wide (blanket) overhead rates' and 'Budgeted overhead rates' in Chapter 4 for the answers to these questions.

(a) (i) and (ii) An activity increase of 150 hours (1650 – 1500) results in an increase in total overheads of £675. It is assumed that the increase in total overheads is due entirely to the increase in variable overheads arising from an increase in activity. Therefore the variable overhead rate is £4.50 (£675/150 hours) per machine hour. The cost structure is as follows:

1. Activity level (hours)	1 500	1 650	2 000
2. Variable overheads at £4.50 per hour	£6 750	£7 425	£9 000
3. Total overheads	£25 650	£26 325	£27 900
4. Fixed overheads (3 – 2)	£18 900	£18 900	£18 900

(iii) The fixed overhead rate is £10.50 (£15 − £4.50 variable rate)

normal activity = fixed overheads (£18 900)/fixed overhead rate (£10.50)
= 1800 machine hours

(iv) Under-absorption = 100 machine hours (1800 – 1700) at £10.50 = £1050

(b) (i) A machine hour rate is recommended for the machine department because most of the overheads (e.g. depreciation and maintenance) are likely to be related to machine hours. For non-machine labour-intensive departments, such as the finishing department, overheads are likely to be related to direct labour hours rather than machine hours. Overheads are therefore charged to jobs performed in the finishing department using the direct labour hour method of recovery.

Calculation of overhead rates

	Machining department	Finishing department
Production overhead	£35 280	£12 480
Machine hours	11 200	
Direct labour hours		7 800
Machine hour overhead rate	£3.15	
Direct labour hour overhead rate		£1.60

(ii)

	Machining department (£)	Finishing department (£)
Direct materials		
(189 × 1.1 × £2.35/0.9)	542.85	—
Direct labour[a]		
25 hours × £4	100.00	
28 hours × £4		112.00
Production overhead		
46 machine hours at £3.15	144.90	
28 direct labour hours at £1.60		44.80
	787.75	156.80

Total cost of job = £944.55 (£787.75 + £156.80)

Note
[a]Overtime premiums are charged to overheads, and are therefore not included in the above job cost.

Question 4.24 (a) (i) Calculation of budgeted overhead absorption rates:

Apportionment of overheads to production departments

	Machine shop (£)	Fitting section (£)	Canteen (£)	Machine maintenance section (£)	Total (£)
Allocated overheads	27 660	19 470	16 600	26 650	90 380
Rent, rates, heat and light[a]	9 000	3 500	2 500	2 000	17 000
Depreciation and insurance of equipment[a]	12 500	6 250	2 500	3 750	25 000
	49 160	29 220	21 600	32 400	132 380
Service department apportionment					
Canteen[b]	10 800	8 400	(21 600)	2 400	–
Machine maintenance section	24 360	10 440	–	(34 800)	–
	84 320	48 060	–	–	132 380

Calculation of absorption bases

		Machine shop		Fitting section	
Product	Budgeted production	Machine hours per product	Total machine hours	Direct labour cost per product (£)	Total direct wages (£)
X	4200 units	6	25 200	12	50 400
Y	6900 units	3	20 700	3	20 700
Z	1700 units	4	6 800	21	35 700
			52 700		106 800

Budgeted overhead absorption rates

Machine shop

$$\frac{\text{budgeted overheads}}{\text{budgeted machine hours}} = \frac{£84\,320}{£52\,700}$$

Fitting section

$$\frac{\text{budgeted overheads}}{\text{budgeted direct wages}} = \frac{48\,060}{106\,800}$$

= 1.60 per machine hour
= 45% of direct wages

Notes
[a] Rents, rates, heat and light are apportioned on the basis of floor area. Depreciation and insurance of equipment are apportioned on the basis of book value.
[b] Canteen costs are reapportioned according to the number of employees. Machine maintenance section costs are reapportioned according to the percentages given in the question.

(ii) The budgeted manufacturing overhead cost for producing one unit of product X is as follows:

	(£)
Machine shop: 6 hours at £1.60 per hour	9.60
Fittings section: 450 of £12	5.40
	15.00

(b) The answer should discuss the limitations of blanket overhead rates and actual overhead rates. See 'Blanket overhead rates' and 'Budgeted overhead rates' in Chapter 4 for the answer to this question.

Question 4.25

(a) The service department cost should be reallocated using the following bases:
    Canteen: Number of employees
    Engineering shop: Number of service hours
    Stores: Number of stores orders
The canteen does not receive any services from the other service departments. Therefore the canteen should be reallocated first. The Engineering Shop receives services from the other two service departments and should be reallocated last.

Overhead allocation

Dept.	Basis	M/C	Assemb	Paint shop	Eng shop	Stores	Canteen
		(£)	(£)	(£)	(£)	(£)	(£)
Allocation		180 000	160 000	130 000	84 000	52 000	75 000
Canteen	Employees	27 000	17 000	13 000	10 000	8 000	(75 000)
Stores	Orders	24 000	18 000	12 000	6 000	(60 000)	
Eng. shop	Service hrs	45 000	30 000	25 000	(100 000)		
Total overhead		276 000	225 000	180 000			
Machine hours		9 200					
Direct labour hours			11 250				
Labour cost				£45 000			
Machine hour rate		£30					
Direct labour hour rate		£20					
Direct labour cost rate		400% of direct labour cost					

(b) *Overhead absorption statement*

	M/C	Assembly	Paint shop
	(£)	(£)	(£)
Overhead absorbed[a]	300 000	156 000	140 000
Actual overhead	290 000	167 000	155 000
(Under-) Over-absorption	10 000	(11 000)	(15 000)

Notes
[a] 10 000 machine hours × £30 per hour.
 7800 Direct labour hours at £20 per hour.
 400% of direct labour cost of £35 000.

(c) See 'Budgeted overhead rates' in Chapter 4 for an explanation of why overheads should be absorbed using predetermined bases. The second part of the question relates to whether or not volume allocation base (i.e. machine hours and direct labour hours or cost) are appropriate, particularly when direct labour is a small proportion of total cost. The answers should discuss the need for developing non-volume-based cost driver rates using activity-based costing systems.

Question 4.26 (a) To calculate product cost, we must calculate overhead absorption rates for the production departments. You can see from the question that the service departments serve each other, and it is therefore necessary to use the repeated distribution method or the simultaneous equation method to reallocate the service department costs. Both methods are illustrated below:

	Cutting (£)	Machining (£)	Pressing (£)	Engineering (£)	Personnel (£)
Allocation per question	154 482	64 316	58 452	56 000	34 000
Engineering reallocation	11 200 (20%)	25 200 (45%)	14 000 (25%)	(56 000)	5 600 (10%)
Personnel reallocation	21 780 (55%)	3 960 (10%)	7 920 (20%)	5 940 (15%)	(39 600)
Engineering reallocation	1 188 (20%)	2 673 (45%)	1 485 (25%)	(5 940)	594 (10%)
Personnel reallocation	327 (55%)	59 (10%)	119 (20%)	89 (15%)	(594)
Engineering reallocation[a]	20	44	25	(89)	
	188 997	96 252	82 001	—	—

Note
[a]The costs are so small that any further apportionments are not justified. Consequently a return charge of 15% is not made to the engineering department and the costs are apportioned in the ratio 55: 10: 20.

Simultaneous equation method
Let
E = total overhead allocated to engineering department
and
P = total overhead allocated to personnel department
Then
$E = 56\,000 + 0.15P$
$P = 34\,000 + 0.10E$

Rearranging the above equations,

$$E - 0.15P = 56\,000 \qquad (1)$$
$$-0.10E + P = 34\,000 \qquad (2)$$

Multiplying equation (2) by 0.15 and equation (1) by 1,

$$E - 0.15P = 56\,000$$
$$-0.015E + 0.15P = 5\,100$$

Adding these equations,

$$0.985E = 61\,100$$
and so $$E = £62\,030$$

Substituting for E in equation (1),

$$62\,030 - 0.15P = 56\,000$$
$$6030 = 0.15P$$
and so $$P = 40\,200$$

We now apportion the values of E and P to the production departments in the agreed percentages:

	Cutting (£)	Machining (£)	Pressing (£)
Allocation per question	154 482	64 316	58 452
Allocation of engineering	12 408(20%)	27 914(45%)	15 508(25%)
Allocation of personnel	22 110(55%)	4 020(10%)	8 040(20%)
	189 000	96 250	82 000

Overhead absorption rates

A comparison of the machine and direct labour hours in the machine department indicates that machine hours are the dominant activity. Therefore a machine hour rate should be used. A direct labour hour rate is appropriate for the cutting and pressing departments. Note that unequal wage rates apply in the cutting department, but equal wage rates apply in the pressing department. The direct wages percentage and the direct labour hour methods will therefore result in identical overhead charges to products passing through the pressing department, and either method can be used. Because of the unequal wage rates in the cutting department, the direct wages percentage method is inappropriate.

The calculation of the overhead absorption rates are as follows:

		(hours)
Cutting:	Product A (4000 × 9 hours)	36 000
	Product B (3000 × 6 hours)	18 000
	Product C (6000 × 5 hours)	30 000
	Total	84 000

$$\text{Absorption rate} = \frac{\pounds189\,000}{84\,000} = \pounds2.25 \text{ per direct labour hour}$$

Machining:	Product A (4000 × 2)	8 000
	Product B (3000 × $1\frac{1}{2}$)	4 500
	Product C (6000 × $2\frac{1}{2}$)	15 000
		27 500

$$\text{Absorption rate} = \frac{\pounds96\,250}{27\,500} = \pounds3.50 \text{ per machine hour}$$

Pressing:	Product A (4000 × 2)	8 000
	Product B (3000 × 3)	9 000
	Product C (6000 × 4)	24 000
		41 000

$$\text{Absorption rate} = \frac{\pounds82\,000}{41\,000} = \pounds2 \text{ per direct labour hour}$$

Product cost calculations

		A (fully complete) (£)	B (partly complete) (£)
Direct materials		7.00	4.00
Direct labour: Cutting	(Skilled)	12.00 (3 × £4)	20.00 (5 × £4)
	(Unskilled)	15.00 (6 × £2.50)	2.50 (1 × £2.50)
	Machining	1.50 ($\frac{1}{2}$ × £3)	0.75 ($\frac{1}{4}$ × £3)
	Pressing	6.00 (2 × £3)	—
Prime cost		41.50	27.25
Overhead:	Cutting	20.25 (9 × £2.25)	13.50 (6 × £2.25)
	Machining	7.00 (2 × £3.50)	5.25 (1$\frac{1}{2}$ × £3.50)
	Pressing	4.00 (2 × £2)	—
		72.75	46.00
		a(i)	a(ii)

(b) The accounting entries for overheads are presented in Chapter 5. You will find when you read this chapter that a credit balance in the overhead control account represents an over recovery of overheads. Possible reasons for this include:

(i) actual overhead expenditure was less than budgeted expenditure;
(ii) actual production activity was greater than budgeted production activity.

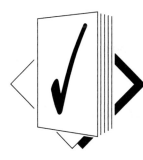

Accounting entries for a job costing system

Solutions to Chapter 5 questions

Question 5.1

Answer = B

Question 5.2

Answer = D

Question 5.3

The profits in the financial accounts exceed the profits in the cost accounts by £4 958 (£79 252 – £74 294). A stock increase represents a reduction in the cost of sales and thus an increase in profits. Therefore the stock increase in the financial accounts must have been £4958 greater than the increase in the cost accounts. The stock increase in the cost accounts was £13 937 (£24 053 – £10 116) so the increase in the financial accounts was £18 895 (£13 937 + £4 958). Thus, the closing stock in the financial accounts was £28 112 (£9 217 + £18 895).

Answer = D

Question 5.4

In the financial accounts there is a total stock decrease of £2900 (£1000 materials and £1900 finished goods) and a decrease of £3200 in the costs accounts (£1200 materials and £2000 finished goods). Since a stock decrease represents an increase in cost of goods sold and a decrease in profits the cost accounting profit will be £300 less than the financial accounting profit. In other words, the financial accounting profit will be £300 greater than the cost accounting profit.

Answer = A

Question 5.5 (a)

Stores ledger control account

	(£)		(£)
Opening Balance	60 140	Finished Goods Control A/c (1)	95 200
Cost Ledger Control A/c	93 106	Closing Balance	58 046
	153 246		153 246

Production wages control account

	(£)		(£)
Cost Ledger Control A/c (2)	121 603	Finished Goods Control A/c	87 480
		Production Overhead	
		Control A/c (2)	34 123
		(indirect wages)	
	121 603		121 603

Production overhead control account

	(£)		(£)
Cost Ledger Control A/c	116 202	Finished Goods Control A/c (3)	61 236
Production Wages		Profit & Loss A/c – Fixed	
Control A/c (2)	34 123	Overhead (3)	90 195
Profit & Loss A/c – over			
absorbed variable			
production overhead (3)	1 106		
	151 431		151 431

Finished goods control account

	(£)		(£)
Opening Balance	147 890	Variable Production Cost of	
Stores Ledger Control A/c	95 200	Sales A/c (balance)	241 619
Production Wages Control A/c	87 480	Closing Balance	150 187
Production Overhead			
Control A/c	61 236		
	391 806		391 806

Workings
(1)

	(Kg)	(£)
Opening stock	540	7 663
Purchases	1 100	15 840
	1 640	23 503

Issue price £23 503/1 640 = £14.33 per kg
Cost of material issues: Material Y = £14.33 × 1 164kg = £16 680
                          Other materials   = £78 520
                                                     £95 200

(2) *Analysis of wages*

	Direct labour (£)	Indirect labour (£)
Direct workers productive time (11 664 × £7.50)	87 480	
Direct workers unproductive time at £7.50 (12 215 hours – 11 664)		4 132.50
Overtime premium (1 075 hours × £2.50)		2 687.50
Indirect workers basic time (4 655 hours × £5.70)		26 533.50
Indirect workers overtime premium (405 hours × £1.90)		769.50
	87 480	34 123.00

Total wages for the period £121 603 (£87 480 + £34 123)

(3) *Analysis of overheads*

Production overheads	= £150 325 (£116 202 + £34 123)
Fixed overheads	= 90 195 (60% × £150 325)
Variable overheads	= 60 130 (40% × £150 325)
Variable overheads absorbed	= 61 236 (70% of the direct labour cost of £87 480)
Over-absorbed overheads	= 1 106 (£61 236 – £60 130)

Note that with a marginal costing system fixed overheads are charged directly to the profit and loss account and not included in the product costs. Therefore they are not included in the finished stocks.

(b) See working (2) in part (a) for the answer to this question.

(c)

	(£)	(£)
Sales		479 462
Less: Variable production cost of sales	241 619	
Variable selling and administration overheads	38 575	
Over-absorbed variable production overheads	(1 106)	279 088
Contribution		200 374
Less: Fixed production overheads	90 195	
Fixed selling and administration overheads	74 360	164 655
Net profit		35 819

Question 5.9

(a) (i)

Raw materials stock account

	(£)		(£)
Opening stock (110 − 7)	103	Issues (difference)	578
Purchases	640	Returns (to supplier)	20
		Closing stock (130 + 15)	145
	743		743

(ii)

Work in progress account

	(£)		(£)
Opening stock (25 + 3)	28	Finished goods a/c (difference)	984
Raw materials a/c	578	Closing stock (27 – 5)	22
Direct labour (220 + 20)	240		
Production overhead absorbed (240 at 66⅔%)	160		
	1006		1006

(iii)

Finished goods account

	(£)		(£)
Opening stock (82 – 9)	73	Cost of sales a/c (difference)	989
Work in progress a/c	984	Closing stock (72 – 4)	68
	1057		1057

(iv)

Profit and loss account

	(£)		(£)
Sales returns a/c	30	Sales a/c	1530
Cost of sales a/c	989		
Gross profit c/d	511		
	1530		1530
Production overheads under absorbed	2	Gross profit b/d	511
Administration expenses	200		
Net profit	309		
	511		511

The reconciliation statement indicates that discounts, selling expenses and debenture interest are not included in the cost accounts. Therefore these items are not included in the costing profit and loss account.

(b) Interest on capital tied up in stocks should be taken into account for decision-making and cost control purposes. This is because the interest on capital tied up in stocks represents an opportunity cost (in terms of the lost interest) which would have been earned if the money tied up in stocks had been invested.

Interest on capital tied up in stocks should not be included in product costs for stock valuation purposes per SSAP 9. Therefore the cost accumulation system will not include notional costs for stock valuation purposes. Nevertheless it is essential that all *relevant* costs (including opportunity costs) are included in cost statements for the purpose of decision-making and cost control.

Question 5.11 (a)

Stores ledger card

Date		Kilos	Total value (£)	Average price per kilo (£)	
Opening balance		21 600	28 944	1.34	
1	Issue	(7 270)	(9 742)	1.34	
7	Purchase	17 400	23 490		
		31 730	42 692	1.3455	(£42 692/31 730)
8	Issue	(8 120)	(10 925)	1.3455	
15	Issue	(8 080)	(10 872)	1.3455	
20	Purchase	19 800	26 730		
		35 330	47 625	1.348	(£47 625/35 330)
22	Issue	(9 115)	(12 287)	1.348	
Closing balance		26 215	35 338	1.348	

Summary of transactions

	(£)
Opening balance	28 944
Purchases	50 220
Issues	(43 826)
Closing balance	35 338

Raw material stock control account

	(£)		(£)
Opening balance	28 944	WIP	43 826
Purchases	50 220	Closing balance	35 338
	79 164		79 164

Production costs for the period:		(£)
Raw materials		43 826
Labour and overhead		35 407
		79 233
Cost per unit (£79 233/17 150 units)		£4.62

Units sold = opening stock (16 960) + production (17 150)
              − closing stock (17 080) = 17 030 units

Finished goods stock control account

	(£)		(£)
Opening balance	77 168	Cost of sales	
Raw materials	43 826	(difference/balancing figure)	77 491
Labour and overhead	35 407	Closing balance	
		(17 080 × £4.62)	78 910
	156 401		156 401

(b) The financial ledger control account is sometimes described as a cost control account or a general ledger adjustment account. For an explanation of the purpose of this account see 'Interlocking accounting' in Chapter 5.

(c) Budgeted production (units):

Sales	206 000	
Add closing stock	18 128	(206 000 × 1.10 × 20/250)
Less opening stock	(17 080)	
	207 048	units

For month 12 the raw material usage is 1.90 kilos per unit of output:

(7270 + 8120 + 8080 + 9115 = 32 585 kg used)/17 150 units produced
∴ Budgeted material usage = 207 048 units × 1.9 kg per unit
                          = 393 391 kg

Budgeted material purchases

Budgeted usage	393 391 kg	
Add closing stock	22 230	(11 700 × 1.9)
Less opening stock	(26 215)	
	389 406 kg	

(a)

Raw material stock control account

	(£)		(£)
Opening balance	72 460	Finished goods (1)	608 400
Creditors	631 220	Closing balance	95 280
	703 680		703 680

Production overhead control account

	(£)		(£)
Bank/Creditors	549 630	Finished goods (3)	734 000
Wages (2)	192 970	P & L – under absorption (3)	8 600
	742 600		742 600

Finished goods stock control account

	(£)		(£)
Opening balance	183 560	Production cost of sales (6)	1 887 200
Raw materials	608 400	Closing balance	225 960
Wages (5)	587 200		
Production overhead	734 000		
	2 113 160		2 113 160

Workings

(1) Raw materials issues:
    Product A: 41 000 units at £7.20 per unit   = £295 200
    Product B: 27 000 units at £11.60 per unit = £313 200

                                         £608 400

(2) Indirect labour charged to production overhead:
    3 250 overtime premium hours at £2 per hour = £6 500 + £186 470 = £192 970

(3) Production overhead absorbed charged to finished goods:
    Product A: 41 000 × 1 hour × £10   = £410 000
    Product B: 27 000 × 1.2 hours × £10 = £324 000

                                       £734 000

    Production overhead under-absorbed = £549 630 + £192 970 – £734 000
    = £8 600

(4) Direct labour charge to finished goods stock:
    Product A: 41 000 × 1 hour × £8   = £328 000
    Product B: 27 000 × 1.2 hours × £8 = £259 200

                                       £587 200

(5) Production cost of sales:
    Cost of product A = £7.20 materials + £8 direct labour + £10 overhead
              = £25.20
    Cost of product B = £11.60 materials + £9.60 direct labour (1.2 hours × £ 8)
                + £12 overhead (1.2 hours × £10) = £33.20
    Cost of sales: Product A = 38 000 units × £25.20 per unit = £957 600
                   Product B = 28 000 units × £33.20 per unit = £929 600

                                    £1 887 200

(6) Valuation of closing stocks of finished goods:
    Product A: 6 200 units at £25.20 = £156 240
    Product B: 2 100 units at £33.20 =   £69 720

                                 £225 960

The above figure can also be derived from the balance of the account.

(b)

	Product A	Product B	Total
	(£000)	(£000)	(£000)
Sales	1330	1092	2422
Production cost of sales	(957.6)	(929.6)	(1887.2)
Gross profit (before adjustment)	372.4	162.4	534.8
Under absorbed production overheads			(8.6)
Gross profit (after adjustment)			526.2
Non-production overheads			(394.7)
Net profit			131.5

(c) With a marginal costing system fixed production overheads are charged directly against profits whereas with an absorption costing system they are included in the product costs and therefore included in the stock valuations. This means that with absorption costing cost of sales and profits will be affected by the changes in stocks. An increase in stocks will result in some of the fixed overheads incurred during the period being deferred to future periods whereas with a decrease in stocks the opposite situation will apply. Thus, absorption costing profits will be higher than marginal costing profits when stocks increase and lower when stocks decrease. For a more detailed explanation of the difference in profits you should refer to 'Variable costing and absorption costing: a comparison of their impact on profit' in Chapter 8.

In this question there is a stock increase of 3000 units for product A resulting in absorption costing profits exceeding marginal costing profits by £20 400 (3000 units at £6.80 per unit fixed overhead). Conversely, for product B there is a 1000 units stock reduction resulting in marginal costing profits exceeding the absorption costing profits by £8160 (1000 units at £8.16 per unit fixed overhead). The overall impact is that absorption costing profits exceed marginal costing profits by £12 240.

(a) A wages control account is a summary account which records total wages payable including employers' national insurance contributions. The account is cleared by a credit and corresponding debits in respect of total wages costs charged to WIP and the overhead control account. The detail which supports the control account is maintained in subsidiary payroll records. **Question 5.13**

(b) (i)

	Dr (£)	Cr (£)
Wages control	122 300	
Bank		122 300
Wages control	58 160	
Employees' National Insurance		14 120
Employees' pension fund contributions		7 200
Income tax		27 800
Court order retentions		1 840
Trade union subscriptions		1 200
Private health plans		6 000
	180 460	180 460
Production overhead control Dr	18 770	
Employer's National Insurance		18 770
	18 770	18 770

(ii)

Work-in-progress control:		
Wages	77 460	
Overtime wages – direct	16 800	
Production overhead control:		
Overtime premium	9 000	
Shift premium	13 000	
Indirect wages	38 400	
Overtime wage – indirect	10 200	
Warehouse construction account	2 300	
Statutory sick pay	9 000	
Idle time	4 300	
Wages control		180 460
	180 460	180 460

Question 5.15 (a) *Calculation of gross wages:*

	Direct workers			Indirect workers			Total
			(£)			(£)	(£)
Attendance time	2640 × 5.00	=	13 200	940 × 4.00	=	3760	
Overtime premium	180 × 2	=	360	75 × 1.60	=	120	
Group bonuses			2 840			710	
Gross wages			16 400			4590	20 990

(b) *Analysis of gross wages:*

	Direct charge (to WIP)			Indirect charge to production overhead			Total
			(£)			(£)	(£)
Attendance time:							
Direct workers	2515 × 5.00	=	12 575	125 × 5.00	=	625	
Indirect workers				940 × 4.00	=	3760	
Overtime premium:							
Direct workers	72 × 2.00	=	144	108 × 2.00	=	216	
Indirect workers	30 × 1.60	=	48	45 × 1.60	=	72	
Group bonuses							
Direct workers						2840	
Indirect workers						710	
			12 767			8223	20 990

Wages control account

	(£)		(£)
Cost ledger control	20 990	Work in progress	12 767
(Gross wages)		Production overhead	8 223
	20 990		20 990

Production overhead control account:

	(£)
Wages control	8223
Cost ledger control	1865
(Employers' employment costs)	

(a) (i) The overheads apportioned to Contract ABC are as follows:
Stores operations = £1.56 million × (£6.4 million × 6 months)/(76.2 million × 53 months) = £148 000
Contract general management = £1.22 million × (£1.017 million/9.762 million) = £127 000
Transport = £1.37 million × (23km × 6 months)/(16km × 53 months) = £223 000
General administration = £4.25 million × (6 months/53 months) = £481 000
Total overheads apportioned to Contract ABC = £979 000

(ii)

	(£ million)	(£ million)
Costs to 1.12.01		1.063
Additional costs from 1.12.01 to 31.5.02:		
Raw materials	1.456	
Direct labour	1.017	
Overheads	0.979	3.452
Costs to date		4.515
Costs to complete		0.937
Total costs		5.452
Contract value		6.400
Estimated contract profit		0.948

Amount of profit taken to be included in the profit statement for the period:

[Value of work certified (£5.18 million)/Contract value (£6.4 million)] × £0.948 million = £0.767 million

Note that with some questions on contract costing the profit to date is computed by deducting the cost of work certified from the value of work certified. However, the cost of work not yet certified or the cost of work certified is not given in the question so it is not possible to adopt this approach.

(b) Service costing represents a costing system where the cost objects are the cost of services rather than the cost of products. It is applied in the service sector but can be applied in other sectors where the objective is to calculate the cost of the service departments. The key factors to consider are as follows:
- determining which services are to be costed within the stores department (e.g. materials receiving, materials handling, etc.);
- establishing whether total costs or unit costs should be calculated. In the latter situation the output should be measurable to calculate the cost per unit of output;
- establishing how costs should be classified in determining the total costs of services (e.g. determining the different categories of direct and indirect costs to be reported);
- deciding the key financial and non-financial performance measures to be reported.

Contract accounts (for the previous year)

	MNO (£000)	PQR (£000)	STU (£000)		MNO (£000)	PQR (£000)	STU (£000)
Materials on site b/fwd			25	Wages accrued b/fwd		2	
Plant on site b/fwd		35	170	Plant control a/c		8	
Materials control a/c	40	99	180	Materials on site c/fwd	8		
Wages control a/c	20	47	110	Plant on site c/fwd	70		110
Subcontractors a/c			35	Prepayment c/fwd			15
Salaries	6	20	25	Cost of work not certified			
Plant control a/c	90	15		c/fwd			26
Wages accrued c/fwd		5		Cost of work certified			
Apportionment of				(balance)[c]	82	221	416
construction services[a]	4	10	22				
	160	231	567		160	231	567
Cost of work certified b/fwd	82	221	416	Attributable sales revenue	82	200	530
Profit taken this period[b]			114	Loss taken[b]		21	
	82	221	530		82	221	530
Cost of work not certified				Wages accrued b/fwd		5	
b/fwd			26				
Materials on site b/fwd	8						
Plant on site b/fwd	70		110				
Prepayment b/fwd			15				

Notes

[a]Costs incurred by construction services department:

	(£000)
Plant depreciation (12 – 5)	7
Salaries	21
Wages paid	8
	36

Wages incurred by each department are:

	(£000)
MNO	20
PQR	50 (47 + 5 − 2)
STU	110
	180

The costs apportioned to each contract are:

	(£000)
MNO	$4\left(\dfrac{[20]}{180} \times £36\right)$
PQR	$10\left(\dfrac{[50]}{180} \times £36\right)$
STU	$22\left(\dfrac{110}{180} \times £36\right)$
	36

[b]See (b) (i) for calculation.

[c]Profit taken plus cost of sales for the current period or cost of sales less loss to date.

(b) (i) *Contract MNO*: Nil.
Contract PQR:

	(£)
Cost of contract to date (see part (a))	411 000
Value of work certified	390 000
Recommended loss to be written off	21 000

Contract STU:

	(£)
Cost of work certified	786 000
Cost of work not yet certified	26 000
Estimated costs to complete	138 000
Estimated cost of contract	950 000
Contract price	1 100 000
Anticipated profit	150 000

The profit taken to date is calculated using the following formula:

$$\frac{\text{cash received to date (£950 000)}}{\text{contract price (£1 100 000)}} \times \text{estimated profit from the contract (£150 000)}$$

$= £129\,545$ (say £129 000)

The profit taken for the current period is £114 000, consisting of the profit to date of £129 000 less the profit previously transferred to the profit and loss account of £15 000.

(ii) *Contract MNO*: This contract is at a very early stage, and it is unlikely that the outcome can be reasonably foreseen. It is therefore prudent not to anticipate any profit at this stage.

Contract PQR: This contract has incurred a loss, and, applying the prudence concept, this loss should be written off as soon as it is incurred.

Contract STU: Applying the prudence concept, a proportion of the profit

$$\frac{\text{cash received to date}}{\text{contract price}}$$

is recognized in this period. The proportion of profit that is recognized is arbitrary and very much a matter of opinion. Alternative apportionments applying the concept of prudence could have been applied.

Process costing

Solutions to Chapter 6 questions

Question summary

6.1–6.6	Multiple choice questions.	6.14–6.20	Problems similar to 6.12 and 6.13, with
6.7–6.10	An explanation of the accounting for		losses in process apportioned between
	normal and abnormal losses.		work in progress and completed
	Preparation of process accounts when		production. Questions 6.15–6.17
	there is no opening or closing WIP.		involve a loss in process which
	Consequently the problem of equivalent		generates sales revenues. Questions
	production does not arise.		6.17, 6.18 and 6.20 involve abnormal
6.11	Preparation of process accounts		gains and 6.17 also involves
	requiring the calculation of equivalent		accounting entries for an integrated
	production and cost per equivalent unit		accounting system.
	using the weighted average basis	6.21	Preparation of process accounts with
	where normal or abnormal losses do		normal and abnormal losses not
	not apply.		requiring equivalent production
6.12–6.13	Calculation of equivalent production		calculations plus a description of
	and cost per equivalent unit using the		weighted average and FIFO methods of
	weighted average basis. Both		stock valuation.
	problems include normal losses in	6.22–6.24	Calculation of the cost per equivalent
	process that are charged only to		unit using the FIFO basis.
	completed production.		

Question 6.1 Answer = A

Question 6.2 Answer = C

Question 6.3 Closing stock = Opening stock (Nil) + Input (13 500) − Completed units (11 750)
= 1750 units

It is assumed that materials are fully complete (£5.75) and labour and overheads are partly complete (£2.50)

Value of closing stock = (1750 × £5.75) + (1750 × £2.50) = £14 437.50

Answer = B

Question 6.4

Actual input	2500	kgs
Normal wastage (10%)	250	
Abnormal loss	75	
Balance = Good production	2175	

Answer = A

Equivalent units (FIFO) **Question 6.5**

	Completed units less opening WIP equiv. units	Closing WIP equiv. units	Abnormal loss equiv.units[a]	Total equiv. units
Materials	23 000 (24 000 – 1000)	3500	500	27 000
Conversion cost	23 300 (24 000 – 700)	2800 (80%)	300 (60%)	26 400

Note
[a] Total input (30 000 + 1000) – ((30 000 × 10%) + 24 000 + 3500) = 500

It is assumed that the answer should adopt the short-cut method and ignore the normal loss in the cost per unit calculation.

(a) Answer = (iii)

(b) Answer = (i)

Input = Opening WIP (2400) + Material input (58 000) = 60 400 litres **Question 6.6**
Output = Completed units (52 500) + Normal loss (5% × 58 000 = 2900) + Closing WIP (3000) = 58 400
Abnormal loss = 60 400 – 58 400 = 2000 litres

It is assumed that the short-cut method described in Appendix 6.1 is adopted whereby the normal loss is not included in the equivalent units calculation. The computation of equivalent units is as follows:

Cost element	Completed units	Abnormal loss equivalent units	Closing WIP equivalent units	Total equivalent units
Materials	52 500	2 000	3 000	57 500
Conversion cost	52 500	2 000	1 500	56 000

Answer = D

(a) (i) **Question 6.10**

Process A account

	(kg)	(£)		(kg)	(£)	(£)
Direct material	2000	10 000	Normal loss	400	0.50	200
Direct labour		7 200	Process B	1400	18.575	26 005
Process costs		8 400	Abnormal loss	200	18.575	3 715
Overhead		4 320				
	2000	29 920		2000		29 920

Unit cost = (£29 920 − £200)/1600 = £18.575

(ii)

Process B account

	(kg)	(£)		(kg)	(£)	(£)
Process A	1400	26 005	Finished goods	2620	21.75	56 989
Direct material	1400	16 800	Normal loss	280	1.825	511
Direct labour		4 200	(10% × 2800)			
Overhead		2 520				
Process costs		5 800				
		55 325				
Abnormal gain	100	2 175				
	2900	57 000		2900		57 500

Unit cost = (£55 325 − £511)/(2800 − 280) = £21.75

(iii)

Normal loss/gain account

	(kg)	(£)		(kg)	(£)
Process A	400	200	Bank (A)	400	200
Process B	280	511	Abnormal gain (B)	100	182.5
			Bank (B)	180	328.5
	680	711		680	711

(iv)

Abnormal loss/gain

	(£)		(£)
Process A	3715	Process B	2175
Normal loss/gain (B)	182.5	Bank	100
		Profit & Loss	1622.5
	3897.5		3897.5

(v)

Finished goods

	(£)		(£)
Process B	56 989		

(vi)

Profit and loss account (extract)

	(£)		(£)
Abnormal loss/gain	1622.5		

Question 6.11 (a)

Units completed = 8250 − Closing WIP (1600) = 6650

Calculation of number of equivalent units produced

	Completed units	Closing WIP	Total equivalent units
Previous process	6650	1600	8250
Materials	6650	1600	8250
Labour and overhead	6650	960 (60%)	7610

(b)

		Total equivalent units	Cost per unit
	(£)		(£)
Previous process cost	453 750	8250	55
Materials	24 750	8250	3
Labour and overheads	350 060	7610	46
			104

(c)

Process account

	Units	(£)		Units	(£)
Input from previous process	8250	453 750	Finished goods[a]	6650	691 600
			Closing WIP[b]	1600	136 960
Materials		24 750			
Labour and overheads		350 060			
	8250	828 560		8250	828 560

Note

[a] Cost of completed production = 6650 units × £104 = £691 600

[b]

		(£)
Closing WIP: Previous process cost (1600 × £55) =		88 000
Materials (1600 × £3)	=	4 800
Labour and overhead (960 × £46)	=	44 160
		136 960

(d) See the introduction to Chapter 7 and 'Accounting for by-products' in Chapter 7 for the answer to this question.

(a) *Production statement*

Input		Output	
Opening stock	3 400	Finished stock	36 000
Input	37 000	WIP	3 200
		Normal loss	1 200
	40 400		40 400

Cost statement

	Opening stock (£)	Current cost (£)	Total cost (£)	Completed units (£)	Normal loss (£)	WIP equivalent units (£)	Total equivalent units	Cost per unit (£)	WIP (£)
Materials	25 500	276 340	301 840	36 000	1200	3200	40 400	7.47	23 904
Conversion cost	30 600	336 000	366 600	36 000	1200	1600	38 800	9.45	15 120
			668 440					16.92	39 024

Normal loss (1200 × £16.92)	20 304	
Completed units (36 000 × £16.92)	609 112	629 416
		668 440

The question does not indicate at what stage in the production process the normal loss is detected. It is assumed that the normal loss is detected at the end of the production process, consequently it is not allocated to WIP. Therefore the total cost of production transferred to finished stock is £629 416.

If the short-cut method described in the Appendix to Chapter 6 is adopted and the normal loss equivalent units are excluded from the above unit cost calculations, the closing WIP valuation is £40 240 and the value of completed production is £628 200. This is equivalent to the following calculation, which apportions the normal loss between completed production and WIP on the basis of equivalent production:

	Completed production (£)	WIP (£)
Materials normal loss		
(1200 × £7.47 = £8964)	8232 (36 000/39 200)	732 (3200/39 200)
Conversion cost normal loss		
(1200 × £9.45 = £11 340)	10 857 (36 000/37 600)	483 (1600/37 600)
Normal loss allocation	19 089	1 215
WIP per cost statement		39 024
Completed production	609 112	
	628 201	40 239

(b) The following characteristics distinguish process costing from job costing:

(i) The cost per unit of output with a process costing system is the average cost per unit, whereas job costing traces the actual cost to each individual unit of output.

(ii) Job costing requires that a separate order and job number be used to collect the cost of each individual job.

(iii) With a process costing system, each unit of output is similar, whereas with a job costing system each unit of output is unique and requires different amounts of labour, material and overheads.

(iv) With a job costing system, costs are accumulated for each order and WIP is calculated by ascertaining the costs that have been accumulated within the accounting period. With a process costing system, costs are not accumulated for each order and it is necessary to use the equivalent production concept to value WIP.

(v) With a process costing system, the allocation of costs to cost of goods sold and closing stocks is not as accurate, because each cost unit is not separately identifiable. Consequently WIP is estimated using the equivalent production concept.

Question 6.18 (a) The abnormal gains and losses are calculated as follows:

	Process 1 (kg)	Process 2 (kg)
Input:		
Opening WIP	500	200
Materials introduced	10 000	
Transfer from previous process		6800
Total input	10 500	7000
Output:		
Completed units	6 800	4570
Normal loss	3 000	1020
Closing WIP	800	150
Total output	10 600	5740
Difference = (Abnormal gain)/Abnormal loss	(100)	1260

Computation of cost per unit for Process 1 based on the short-cut method (see Appendix 6.1):

Cost element	Opening WIP (£)	Current cost (£)	Total cost (£)	Completed units	Abnormal gain	WIP equiv. units	Total equiv. units	Cost per unit (£)
Materials	500	5 500	6 000	6 800	(100)	800	7 500	0.80
Conversion cost	520	6 500	7 020	6 800	(100)	320	7 020	1.00
			13 020					1.80

Cost of completed units (6800 × £1.80)		12 240
Value of abnormal gain (100 × £1.80)		(180)
Closing WIP: Materials (800 × £0.80)	640	
Conversion cost (320 × £1)	320	960
		13 020

Process 1 account

	(Kg)	(£)		(Kg)	(£)
Opening WIP	500	1 020	Normal loss	3 000	—
Materials	10 000	5 500	Process 2	6 800	12 240
Conversion cost		6 500	Closing WIP	800	960
Abnormal gain	100	180			
	10 600	13 200		10 600	13 200

Computation of cost per unit for Process 2 based on the short-cut method (see Appendix 6.1):

Cost element	Opening WIP (£)	Current cost (£)	Total cost (£)	Completed units	Abnormal loss	WIP equiv. units	Total equiv. units	Cost per unit (£)
Previous process cost	360	12 240	12 600	4 570	1 260	150	5 980	2.1070
Conversion cost	105	7 400	7 505	4 570	1 260	105	5 935	1.2645
			20 105					3.3715

Cost of completed units (4570 × £3.3715)		15 408
Value of abnormal loss (1260 × £3.3715)		4 248
Closing WIP: Previous process cost (150 × £2.1070)	316	
Conversion cost (105 × £1.2645)	133	449
		20 105

Process 2 account

	(Kg)	(£)		(Kg)	(£)
Opening WIP	200	465	Normal loss	1 020	—
Process 1	6 800	12 240	Process 2	4 570	15 408
Conversion cost		7 400	Closing WIP	150	449
			Abnormal loss	1 260	4 248
	7 000	20 105		7 000	20 105

(b) Assuming the April output of Process 1 of 6800kg revenues of £29 920 will be received (6800kg × £4.40). Alternatively, the output could be further processed and assuming a normal loss of 15% the normal output will be 5780kg (6800 × 0.85). The average conversion cost per unit in Process 2 is £1.2645 per unit of normal output. Therefore the total cost of sales for the normal output arising from an input of 6800kg from Process 1 is £7309 (5780kg × £1.2645). Hence the variable cost of sales is £7309 × 0.70 = £5116. The incremental contribution to profits from further processing is:

Expected normal output (5780kg × £6.50)	=	£37 570
Less: incremental costs	=	5 116
Incremental contribution		32 454

Compared with the offer from MZ to purchase the output from Process 1 the company is better off by £2534 (£32 454 – £29 920) if it rejects the offer and undertakes further processing in Process 2.

Other factors to consider are:

- the losses in process. The company will only be better off from further processing if the normal loss of 15% is not significantly exceeded. If an abnormal loss occurs similar to April, sales revenues from the final process will be significantly less than the £37 570 used in the above computation and the company will be better off accepting the offer;
- the likelihood and desirability of MZ becoming a future customer;
- the state of the existing market for Process 2;
- the alternative use of Process 2 facilities;
- the likelihood of being able to eliminate the abnormal losses.

(c) See 'Distinguishing between joint products and by-products' and 'Accounting for by-products' in Chapter 7 for the answer to this question.

Question 6.19 (a) Fully complete production = Input (36 000) − Closing WIP (8000)
= 28 000 kg
Normal loss = 2 800 (10% × 28 000 kg)
Abnormal loss = 800 (Actual loss (3600) − 2800)
Good output = 24 400 (28 000 − 3600)

(b)

	Completed units (£)	Normal loss	Abnormal loss	Closing WIP	Total equiv. units	Cost per unit (£)
Previous process cost	166 000	24 400	2800	800	8000	36 000	4.61111
Conversion cost	73 000	24 400	2800	800	4000	32 000	2.28125
	239 000						6.89236

		(£)	(£)
Completed units (24 400 × £6.89236)		168 174	
Add normal loss (2800 × £6.89236)		19 298	
			187 472
Abnormal loss (800 × £6.89236)			5 514
WIP: Previous process cost	(8000 × £4.61111)	36 889	
Conversion cost	(4000 × £2.28125)	9 125	
			46 014
			239 000

The above computations assume that losses are detected at the end of the process when the units are fully complete. Therefore none of the normal loss is allocated to partly completed units (WIP). There is an argument for allocating the normal loss between completed units and the abnormal loss (see the section on equivalent units and abnormal losses in the appendix to Chapter 6) but it is unlikely to make a significant difference to the answer. Also examination questions are unlikely to require such sophisticated answers.

An alternative approach is to adopt the short-cut method described in Chapter 6. This method allocates the normal loss between completed units, WIP and the abnormal loss. Because the units actually lost are fully complete it is likely that losses are detected on completion. Therefore the short-cut method is not theoretically correct. Nevertheless the computations suggest that it was the examiner's intention that the question should be answered using the short-cut method. The revised answer is as follows:

		Completed units	Abnormal loss	WIP	Total equiv. units	Cost per unit (£)	WIP (£)
	(£)						
Previous process cost	166 000	24 400	800	8000	33 200	5.00	40 000
Conversion cost	73 000	24 400	800	4000	29 200	2.50	10 000
	239 000					7.50	50 000

Completed units (24 400 × £7.50)	183 000
Abnormal loss (800 × £7.50)	6 000
	239 000

Distillation process account

	(kg)	(£)		(kg)	(£)
Input from mixing	36 000	166 000	Finished goods	24 400	183 000
Labour		43 800	Abnormal loss	800	6 000
Overheads		29 200	Normal loss	2 800	–
			Closing WIP	8 000	50 000
	36 000	239 000		36 000	239 000

(c) If the scrapped production had a resale value the resale value would be credited to the process account (thus reducing the cost of the process account). The accounting entries would be as follows:

Dr Cash
Cr Process Account (with sales value of normal loss)
Cr Abnormal Loss Account (with sales value of abnormal loss)

Question 6.21

(a)

Expected output from an input of 39 300 sheets:	3 144 000 cans (39 300 × 80)
Less 1% rejects	31 440 cans
Expected output after rejects	3 112 560 cans

The normal loss arising from the rejects (31 440 cans) is sold at £0.26 per kg. It is therefore necessary to express the rejects in terms of kilos of metal. Each sheet weighs 2 kilos but wastage in the form of offcuts is 2% of input. Therefore the total weight of 80 cans is 1.96 kg (0.98 × 2 kg) and the weight of each can is 0.0245 kilos (1.96 kg/80 cans). The weight of the normal loss arising from the rejects is 770.28 kg (31 440 × 0.0245 kg). The normal loss resulting from the offcuts is 1572 kg (39 300 × 2 kg × 0.02). Hence the total weight of the normal loss is 2342.28 kilos (1572 kg + 770.28 kg), with an expected sales value of £609 (2342.28 kg × £0.26).

Process account

	(£)		(£)
Direct materials		Finished goods	
(39 300 × £2.50)	98 250	(3 100 760 cans × £0.042[a])	130 232
		Normal loss	609
Direct labour and		Abnormal loss	
overheads	33 087	(11 800 kg[b] at £0.042[a])	496
	131 337		131 337

Abnormal loss account

	(£)		(£)
Process account	496	Sale proceeds[c]	75
		Profit and loss account	421
	496		496

Notes

[a]Cost per unit = $\dfrac{£98\,250 + £33\,087 - £609}{\text{expected output (3 112 560 cans)}}$ = £0.042 per can

[b]Expected output (3 112 560) − actual output (3 100 760 cans) = 11 800 cans
[c]Abnormal loss = 11 800 cans (3 112 560 − 3 100 760)
This will yield 289.1 kilos (11 800 × 0.0245 kilos) of metal with a sales value of £75 (289.1 × £0.26).

(b) (i) See 'Opening and closing work in progress' in Chapter 6 for the answer to this question.

(ii) See 'Weighted average method' and 'First in, first out method' in Chapter 6 for the answer to this question.

Question 6.22 (a)

Production statement

Input:		Units
Opening WIP		20 000
Transfer from previous process		180 000
		200 000

Output:		
Closing WIP		18 000
Abnormal loss		60
Completed units (balance)		181 940
		200 000

Statement of equivalent production and calculation of cost of completed production and WIP

	Current costs (£)	Completed units less opening WIP equivalent units	Abnormal loss	Closing WIP equivalent units	Current total equivalent units	Cost per unit (£)
Previous process cost	394 200	161 940	60	18 000	180 000	2.19
Materials	110 520	167 940	60	16 200	184 200	0.60
Conversion cost	76 506	173 940	60	12 600	186 600	0.41
	581 226					3.20

	(£)	(£)
Cost of completed production:		
Opening WIP (given)	55 160	
Previous process cost (161 940 × £2.19)	354 649	
Materials (167 940 × £0.60)	100 764	
Conversion costs (173 940 × £0.41)	71 315	581 888
Cost of closing WIP:		
Previous process cost (18 000 × £2.19)	39 420	
Materials (16 200 × £0.60)	9 720	
Conversion costs (12 600 × £0.41)	5 166	54 306
Value of abnormal loss (60 × £3.20)		192
		636 386

Process 3 account

	(£)		(£)
Opening WIP	55 160	Transfer to finished goods	
Transfer from process 2	394 200	stock	581 888
Materials	110 520	Abnormal loss	192
Conversion costs	76 506	Closing WIP	54 306
	636 386		636 386

(b) Normal losses are unavoidable losses that are expected to occur under efficient operating conditions. They are an expected production cost and should be absorbed by the completed production whereas abnormal losses are not included in the process costs but are removed from the appropriate process account and reported separately as an abnormal loss. See 'Losses in process and partially completed units' in the appendix to Chapter 6 for a more detailed explanation of the treatment of normal losses.

(c) If the weighted average method is used, both the units and value of WIP are merged with current period costs and production to calculate the average cost per unit. The weighted average cost per unit is then applied to all completed units, any abnormal losses and closing WIP equivalent units. In contrast, with the FIFO method the opening WIP is assumed to be the first group of units completed during the current period. The opening WIP is charged separately to completed production, and the cost per unit is based only on current costs and production for the period. The closing WIP is assumed to come from the new units that have been started during the period.

(a) It is assumed that the normal loss occurs at the start of the process and should **Question 6.24** be allocated to completed production and closing WIP. It is also assumed that process 2 conversion costs are not incurred when losses occur. Therefore losses should not be allocated to conversion costs.

Statement of input and output (units)

	Input		Output
Opening WIP	1 200	Completed output	105 400
Transferred from Process 1	112 000	WIP	1 600
		Normal loss (5% × 112,000)	5 600
		Abnormal loss (balance)	600
	113 200		113 200

Since the loss occurs at the start of the process it should be allocated over all units that have reached this point. Thus the normal loss should be allocated to all units of output. This can be achieved by adopting the short-cut method described in Chapter 6 whereby the normal loss is not included in the unit cost statement.

Calculation of cost per unit and cost of completed production (FIFO method)

	Current costs (£)	Completed units less opening WIP equiv. units	Abnormal loss	Closing WIP equiv. units	Current total equiv. units	Cost per unit (£)
Previous process cost	187 704					
Materials	47 972					
	235 676	104 200(105 400 − 1200)	600	1600	106 400	2.215
Conversion costs	63 176	104 800(105 400 − 600)	—	1200	106 000	0.596
	298 852					2.811

Cost of completed production:	(£)	(£)
Opening WIP (given)	3 009	
Previous process cost and materials (104 200 × £2.215)	230 803	
Conversion cost (104 800 × £0.596)	62 461	296 273
Abnormal Loss (600 × £2.215)		1 329
Closing WIP:		
Previous process cost and materials (1600 × £2.215)	3 544	
Conversion costs (1200 × £0.596)	715	4 259
		301 861

Process 2 account

	(£)		(£)
Opening WIP	3 009	Transfer to finished goods	296 273
Transfers from Process 1	187 704	Abnormal loss	1 329
Raw materials	47 972	Closing WIP	4 259
Conversion costs	63 176		
	301 861		301 861

(b) If the loss occurs at the end of the process then the normal loss should only be charged to those units that have reached the end of the process. In other words, the cost of normal losses should not be allocated to closing WIP. To meet this requirement a separate column for normal losses is incorporated into the unit cost statement and the normal loss equivalent units are included in the calculation of total equivalent units. The cost of the normal loss should be calculated and added to the cost of completed production. For an illustration of the approach see 'Losses in process and partially completed units' in the appendix to Chapter 6.

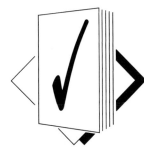

Joint and by-product costing

Solutions to Chapter 7 questions

Question 7.4

(a)

Process 1 account

	(kg)	(£)		(kg)	(£)
Materials	7000	3500	Normal loss (W2)	700	280
Labour and overhead		4340	Transferred to		
Abnormal gain (W3)	130	156	process 2 (W1)	6430	7716
	7130	7996		7130	7996

Workings

(W1)

$$\text{Cost per unit} = \frac{\text{cost of production (£7840)} - \text{scrap value of normal loss (£280)}}{\text{expected output (6300 kg)}}$$

$$= £1.20 \text{ per kg}$$

(W2) Normal loss is 10% of *total* output, which in this case is equivalent to total input [therefore normal loss = $(10\% \times (6430 + 570))$].

(W3) Abnormal gain = actual output (6430) − expected output (6300)

Normal loss account

	(£)		(£)
Process 1		Abnormal	
(700 × £0.40)	280	gain a/c	
		(130 × £0.40)	52
		Cash	
		(570 × £0.40)	228
	280		280

Abnormal gain account

	(£)		(£)
Normal loss		Process 1	156
(130 × £0.40)	52		
P & L a/c	104		
	156		156

Process 2 account

	(kg)	(£)		(kg)	(£)
Previous process cost	6430	7 716	By-product net income	430	645
Labour and overhead		12 129	Output to be account for		19 200
			E	2000	
			F	4000	
	6430	19 845		6430	19 845

The allocation of £19 200 to E and F depends on the apportionment method used.

(i) *Physical output method*

	E (£)	F (£)
1. Total output cost	$6400 \left(\dfrac{2000}{6000} \times £19\,200 \right)$	$12\,800 \left(\dfrac{4000}{6000} \times £19\,200 \right)$
2. Closing stock	$2880 \left(\dfrac{2000 - 1100}{2000} \times £6400 \right)$	$2\,560 \left(\dfrac{4000 - 3200}{4000} \times £12\,800 \right)$
3. Cost of sales	$3520 \left(\dfrac{1100}{2000} \times £6400 \right)$	$10\,240 \left(\dfrac{3200}{4000} \times £12\,800 \right)$
4. Sales revenue	7700 (1100 × £7)	8 000 (3200 × £2.50)
5. Profit (4 − 3)	4180	(2 240)

(ii) *Market value of output method*

	E (£)	F (£)
1. Market value of output	14 000 (2000 × £7)	10 000 (4000 × £2.50)
2. Cost of output	$11\,200 \left(\dfrac{14}{24} \times £19\,200 \right)$	$8\,000 \left(\dfrac{10}{24} \times £19\,200 \right)$
3. Closing stock	$5\,040 \left(\dfrac{[900]}{2000} \times £11\,200 \right)$	$1\,600 \left(\dfrac{[800]}{4000} \times £8\,000 \right)$
4. Cost of sales	$6\,160 \left(\dfrac{1100}{2000} \times £11\,200 \right)$	$6\,400 \left(\dfrac{3200}{4000} \times £8\,000 \right)$
5. Sales revenue	7 700	8 000
6. Profit (5 − 4)	1 540	1 600

(c) See Chapter 7 for the answer to this question. In particular, the answer should stress that joint cost apportionments are necessary for stock valuation, but such apportionments are inappropriate for decision-making. For decision-making relevant costs should be used. It can be seen from the answer to part (b) that one method of apportionment implies that F makes a loss whereas the other indicates that F makes a profit. Product F should only be deleted if the costs saved from deleting it exceed the revenues lost.

(a) Normal loss (toxic waste) = 50 kg per 1000 kg of input (i.e. 5%)
Actual input = 10 000 kg
Abnormal loss = Actual toxic waste (600) less normal loss (500) = 100 kg

By-product R net revenues of £1750 are credited to the joint (main) process account and normal and abnormal losses are valued at the average cost per unit of output:

$$\frac{\text{Net cost of production (£35 750} - \text{£1750)}}{\text{Expected output of the joint products (8500 kg)}} = £4$$

The cost of the output of the joint products is £33 600 (8400 kg × £4) and this is to be allocated to the individual products on the basis of final sales value (i.e. 4800 kg × £5 = £24 000 for P and 3600 kg × £7 = £25 200 for Q):
P = £24 000/£49 200 × £33 600 = £16 390
Q = £25 200/£49 200 × £33 600 = £17 210

The main process account is as follows:

Main process account

	(kg)	(£)		(kg)	(£)
Materials	10 000	15 000	P Finished goods	4 800	16 390
Direct labour	—	10 000	Q Process 2	3 600	17 210
Variable overhead	—	4 000	By-product R	1 000	1 750
Fixed overhead	—	6 000	Normal toxic waste	500	—
Toxic waste disposal a/c	—	750	Abnormal toxic waste	100	400
	10 000	35 750		10 000	35 750

(b)
Toxic waste disposal (Creditors' account)

	(£)		(£)
Bank	900	Main process account	750
		Abnormal toxic waste	150
	900		900

Abnormal toxic waste account

Main process account	400	Profit and Loss Account	550
Toxic waste disposal account (100 × £1.50)	150		
	550		550

Process 2 account

	kg	£		kg	£
Main process Q	3600	17 210	Finished goods Q[b]	3 300	26 465
Fixed cost		6 000	Closing work-in-progress[b]	300	1 920
Variable cost		5 175[a]			
	3600	28 385		3600	28 385

Notes:
[a] 3300 + (50% × 300) × £1.50 = £5175
[b]

	(£)	Completed units	WIP equiv. units	Total equiv. units	Cost per unit
Previous process cost	17 210	3300	300	3600	£4.78
Conversion cost	11 175	3300	150	3450	£3.24
					£8.02

	(£)
Completed units (3 300 units × £8.02)	26 465
WIP (300 × £4.78) + (150 × £3.24)	1 920
	28 385

(c) See the section on methods of apportioning joint costs to joint products in Chapter 6 for the answer to this question.

(d)

	(£)
Incremental sales revenue per kg from further processing (£7 − £4.30)	2.70
Incremental (variable) cost per kg of further processing	1.50
Incremental contribution per kg from further processing	1.20

	(£)
At an output of 3600 kg the incremental contribution is	4320
Avoidable fixed costs	3600
Net benefit	720

$$\text{Break-even point} = \frac{\text{Avoidable fixed costs (£3600)}}{\text{Incremental unit contribution (£1.20)}} = 3000 \text{ kg}$$

Further processing should be undertaken if output is expected to exceed 3000 kg per week.

Question 7.7 (a) See Figure Q7.7

> *Workings*
> (W1)   (4000 + 2600 − 300)/900 = £7
> (W2)   (2100 + 3300)/300 = £18
> (W3)   (1400 + 2400)/200 = £19
> (W4)   (2800 + 1500 + 1155 + 1350 + 1520)/555 = £15

(b)

Product	Output (tonnes)	Total cost (£)	Cost per tonne (£)
XXX	555	8325	15
Y	225	4050	18
Z	120	2280	19

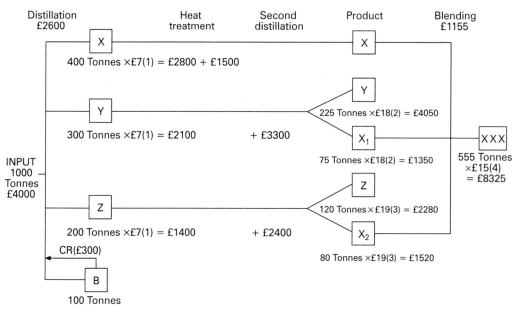

Figure Q7.7

(c) An alternative treatment is to credit the income direct to the profit and loss account rather than crediting the proceeds to the process from which the by-product was derived.

Question 7.9

(a) Operating statement for October 2000

(£)		(£)
Sales: Product A (80 000 × £5) =	400 000	
Product B (65 000 × £4) =	260 000	
Product C (75 000 × £9) =	675 000	1 335 000
Operating costs	1 300 000	
Less closing stock[a]	200 000	
		1 100 000
Profit		235 000

Note
[a] Production for the period (kg):

	A	B	C	Total
Sales requirements	80 000	65 000	75 000	
Closing stock	20 000	15 000	5 000	
Production	100 000	80 000	80 000	260 000

$$\text{Cost per kg} = 260\,000\text{ kg} = \frac{£1\,300\,000}{260\,000} = £5 \text{ per kg}$$

Therefore
$$\text{Closing stock} = 40\,000 \text{ kg at } £5 \text{ per kg}$$

(b) Evaluation of refining proposal

	A	B	C	Total (£)
Incremental revenue per kg (£)	12	10	11.50	
Variable cost per kg (£)	4	6	12.00	
Contribution per kg (£)	8	4	(0.50)	
Monthly production (kg)	100 000	80 000	80 000	
Monthly contribution (£)	800 000	320 000	(40 000)	1 080 000
Monthly fixed overheads (specific to B)		360 000		360 000
Contribution to refining general fixed costs (£)	800 000	(40 000)	(40 000)	720 000
Refining general fixed overheads				700 000
Monthly profit				20 000

1. It is more profitable to sell C in its unrefined state and product B is only profitable in its refined state if monthly sales are in excess of 90 000 kg (£360 000 fixed costs/£4 contribution per unit).
2. If both products B and C are sold in their unrefined state then the refining process will yield a profit of £100 000 per month (£800 000 product A contribution less £700 000 fixed costs).
3. The break-even point for the refining process if only product A were produced is 87 500 kg (£700 000 fixed costs/£8 contribution per unit). Consequently if sales of A declined by 12½%, the refining process will yield a loss. Note that 80 000 kg of A were sold in October.

Question 7.10 (a)

	B (£)	K (£)	C (£)	Total (£)
Revenue	35 000	50 000	60 000	
Pre-separation joint costs (1)	17 500	12 500	10 000	
Post separation costs	20 000	10 000	22 500	
Profit/(loss)	(2 500)	27 500	27 500	52 500

(b)

	B	K	C
Incremental costs	20 000	10 000	22 500
Incremental revenue	14 000	30 000	42 000
Incremental benefit	(6 000)	20 000	19 500

Therefore profit will increase by £6000 if B is sold at split off point and the revised profit statements will be:

Revenue	21 000	50 000	60 000	
Pre-separation costs[a]	17 500	12 500	10 000	
Post separation costs	—	10 000	22 500	
Profit	3 500	27 500	27 500	58 500

Note
[a]B = 3500/8000 × £40 000; K = 2500/8000 × £40 000; C = 2000/8000 × £40 000.

Question 7.14 (a) You can see from the question that the input is 240 000 kg and the output is 190 000 kg. It is assumed that the difference of 50 000 kg is a normal loss in output which occurs at the start of processing. Therefore the loss should be charged to the completed production and WIP. By making no entry for normal losses in the cost per unit calculation the normal loss is automatically apportioned between completed units and WIP.

	Opening WIP (£)	Current cost (£)	Total cost (£)	Completed units	Closing WIP	Total equivalent units	Cost per unit (£)	WIP value (£)
Materials	20 000	75 000	95 000	160 000	30 000	190 000	0.50	15 000
Processing costs	12 000	96 000	108 000	160 000	20 000	180 000	0.60	12 000
			203 000				1.10	27 000
				Completed units (160 000 units × £1.10)				176 000
								203 000

(b) This question requires a comparison of incremental revenues and incremental costs. Note that the costs of process 1 are irrelevant to the decision since they will remain the same whichever of the two alternatives are selected. You should also note that further processing 120 000 kg of the compound results in 240 000 kg of Starcomp.

Incremental sales revenue:

	(£)	(£)
Starcomp (120 000 × 2 kg × £2)	480 000	
Compound (120 000 × £1.60)	192 000	288 000
Incremental costs:		
Materials	120 000	
Processing costs	120 000	240 000
Incremental profits		48 000

It is therefore worthwhile further processing the compound.

(c) The sales revenue should cover the additional costs of further processing the 40 000 kg compound and the lost sales revenue from the 40 000 kg compound if it is sold without further processing.

Additional processing costs:

	(£)
Materials (£160 000 − £120 000)	40 000
Processing costs (£140 000 − £120 000)	20 000
Lost compound sales revenue (40 000 × £1.60)	64 000
	124 000

$$\text{Minimum selling price per kg of Starcomp} = \frac{£124\,000}{40\,000\ \text{kg} \times 2}$$

$$= £1.55$$

(a) *Profit and loss account*

	W (£)	X (£)	Z (£)	Total (£)
Opening stock	—	—	8 640	8 640
Production cost	189 060	228 790	108 750	526 600
Less closing stock	(14 385)	(15 070)	(15 010)	(44 465)
Cost of sales	174 675	213 720	102 380	490 775
Selling and administration costs	24 098	27 768	10 011	61 877
Total costs	198 773	241 488	112 391	552 652
Sales	240 975	277 680	100 110	618 765
Profit/(loss)	42 202	36 192	(12 281)	66 113

Workings

Joint process cost per kilo of output = £0.685 per kg (£509 640/744 000 kg)

Production cost for products W, X and Y:

$$\text{Product W}\ (276\,000\ \text{kg} \times £0.685) = £189\,060$$
$$\text{X}\ (334\,000\ \text{kg} \times £0.685) = £228\,790$$
$$\text{Y}\ (134\,000\ \text{kg} \times £0.685) = £91\,790$$

Closing stocks for products W and X:

$$\text{Product W}\ (21\,000\ \text{kg} \times £0.685) = £14\,385$$
$$\text{X}\ (22\,000\ \text{kg} \times £0.685) = £15\,070$$

Cost per kilo of product Z:

		(£)
Product Y (128 000 kg × £0.685)	=	87 680
Further processing costs		17 920
Less by-product sales (8000 × £0.12)	=	(960)
		104 640
Cost per kilo (£104 640/96 000 kg)		£1.09

Closing stock of product Z (10 000 kg × £1.09)	=	£10 900
Add closing stock of input Y (6000 × £0.685)	=	£4 110
Closing stock relating to product Z		£15 010

Production cost relating to final product Z:

	(£)
Product Y (134 000 kg × £0.685) =	91 790
Further processing costs	17 920
Less by-product costs	(960)
	108 750

(b) The joint costs are common and unavoidable to both alternatives, and are therefore not relevant for the decision under consideration. Further processing from an input of 128 000 kg of Y has resulted in an output of 96 000 kg of Z. Thus it requires 1.33 kg of Y to produce 1 kg of Z (128/96).

	(£)
Revenue per kilo for product Z	1.065 (£100 110/94 000 kg)
Sale proceeds at split-off point (1.33 × £0.62)	0.823
Incremental revenue per kg from further processing	0.242
Incremental costs of further processing	0.177 [(£17 920 − £960)/96 000]
Incremental profit from further processing	0.065

It is assumed that selling and administration costs are fixed and will be unaffected by which alternative is selected. The company should therefore process Y further into product Z and not accept the offer from the other company to purchase the entire output of product Y.

(c) See 'Methods of allocation joint costs to joint products' in Chapter 7 for the answer to this question.

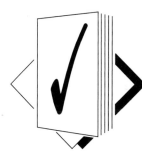

Income effects of alternative cost accumulation systems

Solutions to Chapter 8 questions

Question summary

8.1 Multiple choice question.
8.2–8.3 Essay questions relating to Chapter 8.
8.4–8.13 These questions are appropriate for a first-year course and require absorption costing and variable costing profit calculations and stock valuations. Questions 8.8, 8.12 and 8.13 are the most difficult, and include an explanation of the difference between variable and absorption costing profit calculations. Questions 8.6 and 8.7 also involves CVP analysis and 8.12 requires the preparation of absorption and variable costing statements using both FIFO and average costing methods.

Question 8.1

Answer = B

Question 8.5

(a) Manufacturing cost per unit of output = variable cost (£6.40) + fixed cost (£92 000/20 000 = £4.60) = £11
Absorption costing profit statement

	(£000)
Sales (22 000 units at £14 per unit)	308.0
Manufacturing cost of sales (22 000 units × £11)	242.0
Manufacturing profit before adjustment	66.0
Overhead over-absorbed [a]	4.6
Manufacturing profit	70.6

Note:
[a] The normal activity that was used to establish the fixed overhead absorption rate was 20 000 units but actual production in period 2 was 21 000 units. Therefore a period cost adjustment is required because there is an over-absorption of fixed overheads of £4 600 [(22 000 units – 21 000 units) × £4.60].

(b)

	(£000)
Sales	308.0
Variable cost of sales (22 000 units × £6.40)	140.8
Contribution to fixed costs	167.2
Less fixed overheads	92.0
Profit	75.2

(c) (i) Compared with period 1 profits are £34 800 higher in period 2 (£70 600 – £35 800). The reasons for the change are as follows:

	(£000)
Additional sales (7000 units at a profit of £3 per unit)	21 000
Difference in fixed overhead absorption (3000 units extra production at £4.60 per unit)[a]	13 800
Additional profit	34 800

Note:

[a] Because fixed overheads are absorbed on the basis of normal activity (20 000 units) there would have been an under-recovery of £9200 (2000 units × £4.60) in period 1 when production was 18 000 units. In period 2 production exceeds normal activity by 1000 units resulting in an over-recovery of £4600. The difference between the under- and over-recovery of £13 800 (£9200 + £4600) represents a period cost adjustment that is reflected in an increase in profits of £13 800. In other words, the under-recovery of £9200 was not required in period 2 and in addition there was an over-recovery of £4600.

(c) (ii) Additional profits reported by the marginal costing system are £4600 (£75 200 – £70 600). Because sales exceed production by 1000 units in period 2 there is a stock reduction of 1000 units. With an absorption costing system the stock reduction will result in a release of £4600 (1000 units at £4.60) fixed overheads as an expense during the current period. With a marginal costing system changes in stock levels do not have an impact on the fixed overhead that is treated as an expense for the period. Thus, absorption costing profits will be £4600 lower than marginal costing profits.

Question 8.6 (a)

January	(£)	Marginal costing (£)	(£)	Absorption costing (£)
Sales revenue (7000 units)		315 000		315 000
Less: Cost of sales (7000 units)				
Direct materials	77 000		77 000	
Direct labour	56 000		56 000	
Variable production overhead	28 000		28 000	
Variable selling overhead	35 000	196 000		
Fixed overhead (7000 × £3)			21 000	182 000
Contribution		119 000		
Gross profit				133 000
Over absorption of fixed production overhead (1)				1 500
				134 500
Fixed production costs (2)	24 000			
Fixed selling costs (2)	16 000		16 000	
Variable selling costs			35 000	
Fixed admin costs (2)	24 000	64 000	24 000	75 000
Net profit		55 000		59 500

February	(£)	Marginal costing (£)	(£)	Absorption costing (£)
Sales revenue (8750 units)		393 750		393 750
Less: Cost of sales (8750 units)				
Direct materials	96 250		96 250	
Direct labour	70 000		70 000	
Variable production overhead	35 000		35 000	
Variable selling overhead	43 750	245 000		
Fixed overhead (8750 × £3)			26 250	227 500
Contribution		148 750		
Gross profit				166 250
Under absorption of fixed production overhead				750
				165 500
Fixed production costs (2)	24 000			
Fixed selling costs (2)	16 000		16 000	
Variable selling costs			43 750	
Fixed admin costs (2)	24 000	64 000	24 000	83 750
Net profit		84 750		81 750

Workings:
(1) Fixed production overhead has been unitized on the basis of a normal monthly activity of 8000 units (96 000 units per annum). Therefore monthly production fixed overhead incurred is £24 000 (8000 × £3). In January actual production exceeds normal activity by 500 units so there is an over-absorption of £1500 resulting in a period cost adjustment that has a positive impact on profits. In February production is 250 units below normal activity giving an under-absorption of production overheads of £750.

(2) With marginal costing fixed production overheads are treated as period costs and not assigned to products. Therefore the charge for fixed production overheads is £24 000 per month (see note 1). Both marginal and absorption costing systems treat non-manufacturing overheads as period costs. All of the non-manufacturing overheads have been unitized using a monthly activity level of 8000 units. Therefore the non-manufacturing fixed overheads incurred are as follows:

Selling = £16 000 (8000 × £2)
Administration = £24 000 (8000 × £3)

(b) In January additional profits of £4500 are reported by the absorption costing system. Because production exceeds sales by 1500 units in January there is a stock increase of 1500 units. With an absorption costing system the stock increase will result in £4500 (1500 units × £3) being incorporated in closing stocks and deferred as an expense to future periods. With a marginal costing system changes in stock levels do not have an impact on the fixed overhead that is treated as an expense for the period. Thus, absorption costing profits will be £4500 higher than marginal costing profits. In February sales exceed production by 1000 units resulting in a stock reduction of 1000 units. With an absorption costing system the stock reduction will result in a release of £3000 (1000 units at £3) fixed overheads as an expense during the current period. Thus, absorption costing profits are £3000 lower than marginal costing profits.

(c) (i) Contribution per unit = Selling price (£45) – unit variable cost (£28) = £17
Break-even point (units) = Annual fixed costs (£64 000)/unit contribution (£17)
= 3765 units
Break-even point (£ sales) = 3765 units × £45 selling price = £169 424
The above calculations are on a monthly basis. The sales value of the annual
break-even point is £2 033 100 (£169 425 × 12).

(ii) Required contribution for an annual profit of £122 800
= Fixed costs (£64 000 × 12) + £122 800
= £899 800

Required activity level = Required contribution (£899 800)

────────────────────────────────

Unit contribution (£17)
= 52 400 units

(d) See 'Cost–volume–profit analysis assumptions' in Chapter 9 for the answer to this
question.

Question 8.8 (a) *Preliminary calculations*

	January–June (£)	July–December (£)
Production overheads	90 000	30 000
(Over)/underabsorbed	(12 000)	12 000
	78 000	42 000

Change in overheads	£36 000	
Change in production volume (units)	12 000	
Production variable overhead rate per unit	£3	
Fixed production overheads (£78 000 – (18 000 × £3))	£24 000	
Distribution costs	£45 000	£40 000
Decrease in costs	£5 000	
Decrease in sales volume (units)	5 000	
Distribution cost per unit sold	£1	
Fixed distribution cost (£45 000 – (15 000 × £1))	£30 000	

Unit costs are as follows:

	(£)	(£)
Selling price		36
Direct materials	6	
Direct labour	9	
Variable production overhead	3	
Variable distribution cost	1	19
Contribution		17

Note that the unit direct costs are derived by dividing the total cost by units
produced

Marginal costing profit statement

	January–June		July–December	
	(£000)	(£000)	(£000)	(£000)
Sales		540		360
Variable costs at £19 per unit sold		285		190
Contribution		255		170
Fixed costs:				
Production overhead	24		24	
Selling costs	50		50	
Distribution cost	30		30	
Administration	80	184	80	184
Profit		71		(14)

(b) Marginal costing stock valuation per unit = £18 per unit production variable cost
Absorption costing stock valuation per unit = £20 per unit total production cost

	January–June (£000)	July–December (£000)
Absorption costing profit	77	(22)
Fixed overheads in stock increase of 3000 units	6	
Fixed overheads in stock decrease of 4000 units		(8)
Marginal costing profit	71	14

(c) Absorption gross profit per unit sold = Annual gross profit (£400 000)/Annual production (15 000 units)
= £16

	(£000)
Profit from January–June	77
Reduction in sales volume (5000 × £16)	(80)
Difference in overhead recovery (£12 000 over recovery and £12 000 under recovery)	(24)
Reduction in distribution cost	5
	(22)

(d) Fixed cost £184 000 × 2 = £368 000
Contribution per unit £17
Break-even point 21 647 units (Fixed costs/contribution per unit)

(e) See 'Some arguments in support of variable costing'in Chapter 8 for the answer to this question.

(a) See sections on some arguments in support of variable costing and some **Question 8.10** arguments in support of absorption costing in Chapter 8 for the answer to this question.

(b) (i)

	(£)
Fixed production overhead per unit	= 0.60 (£144 000/240 000 units)
Variable production cost per unit	= 1.30 (£312 000/240 000 units)
Variable selling and administration overhead per unit	= 0.10 (£24 000/240 000 units)
Fixed selling and administration overhead per unit	= 0.40 (£96 000/240 000 units)
	2.40
Selling price	3.00
Profit	0.60

	(£)
Fixed production overhead incurred	144 000
Fixed production overhead absorbed (260 000 × £0.60)	156 000
Over-recovery	£12 000

(ii) *Absorption costing profit*:

	(£)
Opening stock (40 000 × £1.90)	76 000
Production cost (260 000 × £1.90)	494 000
	570 000
Less closing stock (70 000 × £1.90)	133 000
Cost of sales (230 000 × £1.90)	437 000
Less over recovery of fixed production overhead	12 000
	425 000
Selling and administration overhead:	
Variable (230 000 × £0.10)	23 000
Fixed	96 000
Total cost	544 000
Sales (230 000 × £3)	690 000
Profit	£146 000

Marginal costing profit:

	(£)
Contribution (230 000 × (£3 − £1.40))	368 000
Less fixed costs (£144 000 + £96 000)	240 000
Profit	£128 000

(iii)

	(£)
Absorption costing profit	146 000
Fixed overhead included in stock increase (30 000 × £0.60)	18 000
Marginal costing profit	£128 000

(iv) The profit figure will be the same with both systems whenever production equals sales and therefore opening stock equals closing stock.

Question 8.11 (a)

Cost element	Total cost (£)	Completed units	WIP equivalent units	Total equivalent units	Cost per unit (£)	WIP (£)
Materials	714 000	98 000	4000	102 000	7.00	28 000
Labour	400 000	98 000	2000	100 000	4.00	8 000
Variable overhead	100 000	98 000	2000	100 000	1.00	2 000
Fixed overhead	350 000	98 000	2000	100 000	3.50	7 000
	1 564 000				15.50	45 000

(b) *Absorption costing profit statement*:

	(£)	(£)
Sales		1 800 000
Production cost	1 564 000	
Closing WIP	(45 000)	
Closing finished goods stock (8000 × £15.50)	(124 000)	1 395 000
Gross profit		405 000
Less: Variable selling and administration costs (£1.60 × 90 000)		(144 000)
Fixed selling and administration costs		(250 000)
Net profit		£11 000

(c) *Marginal costing profit statement*:

	(£)	(£)
Sales		1 800 000
Variable cost of production	1 214 000	
Closing WIP	(38 000)	
Closing finished goods stock (8000 × £12)	(96 000)	
Variable cost of sales	1 080 000	
Variable selling and administration costs	144 000	1 224 000
Contribution		576 000
Less: Fixed costs (350 + 200 + 50)		(600 000)
Net loss		£(24 000)

(d) The absorption costing statement shows a profit of £11 000 whereas the marginal costing statement shows a net loss of £24 000. The difference of £35 000 is due to the fact that the closing stock valuation includes £35 000 fixed overhead (£7000 WIP and £28 000 finished goods) whereas the fixed overheads are not included in the stock valuation when the marginal costing approach is used. Instead, *all* the fixed overheads are charged as a period cost. With the absorption costing system, the fixed overheads of £35 000 that are included in the stock valuation will be recorded as an expense when the stocks are sold. Consequently, the absorption costing method shows £35 000 greater profits than the marginal costing method. For a detailed discussion of a comparison of the impact on profits of the two methods see Chapter 8.

For internal profit measurement purposes both methods are acceptable, but for external reporting SSAP 9 requires that stocks should be valued on an absorption costing basis.

Question 8.12

(a)
$$\text{Fixed overhead rate per unit} = \frac{\text{Budgeted fixed overheads (£300 000)}}{\text{Budgeted production (40 000 units)}} = \text{£7.50}$$

Absorption Costing (FIFO) Profit Statement:

		(£000)
Sales (42 000 × £72)		3024
Less cost of sales:		
Opening stock (2000 × £30)	60	
Add production (46 000 × £52.50[a])	2415	
	2475	
Less closing stock (6000 × £52.50)	315	2160
		864
Add over-absorption of overheads[b]		27
Profit		891

Notes:
[a] Variable cost per unit = £2070/46 000 = £45
Total cost per unit = £45 + £7.50 Fixed overhead = £52.50
[b] Overhead absorbed (46 000 × £7.50) = £345 000
Actual overhead incurred = £318 000
Over-recovery = £27 000

Marginal Costing (FIFO) Profit Statement:

	(£000)	(£000)
Sales		3024
Less cost of sales:		
Opening stock (2000 × £25)	50	
Add production (46 000 × £45)	2070	
	2120	
Less closing stock (6000 × £45)	270	1850
Contribution		1174
Less fixed overheads incurred		318
Profit		856

Reconciliation:

Absorption profit exceeds marginal costing profit by £35 000 (£891 000 − £856 000). The difference is due to the fixed overheads carried forward in the stock valuations:

	(£)
Fixed overheads in closing stocks (6000 × £7.50)	45 000
Less fixed overheads in opening stocks (2000 × £5)	10 000
Fixed overheads included in stock movement	35 000

Absorption costing gives a higher profit because more of the fixed overheads are carried forward into the next accounting period than were brought forward from the last accounting period.

(b) *Absorption Costing (AVECO) Profit Statement:*

	(£000)	(£000)
Sales		3024
Opening stock plus production		
(48 000 × £51.56[a])	2475	
Less closing stock (6000 × £51.56)	309	2166
		858
Add over-absorption of overheads		27
Profit		885

Marginal Costing (AVECO) Profit Statement:

	(£000)	(£000)
Sales		3024
Less cost of sales		
Opening stock plus production		
(48 000 × £44.17[b])	2120	
Less closing stock (6000 × £44.17)	265	1855
Contribution		1169
Less fixed overheads		318
Profit		851

Notes:

[a] With the AVECO method the opening stock is merged with the production of the current period to ascertain the average unit cost:
Opening stock (2000 × £30) + Production cost (£2 415 000) = £2 475 000
Average cost per unit = £2 475 000/48 000 units
[b] Average cost = (Production cost (£2 070 000) + Opening stock (50 000))/48 000 units.

Reconciliation:

	(£000)
Difference in profits (£885 − £851)	34
Fixed overheads in closing stocks (309 − 265)	44
Less fixed overheads in opening stock (2000 × £5)	10
Fixed overheads included in stock movement	34

The variations in profits between (a) and (b) are £6000 for absorption costing and £5000 for marginal costing. With the FIFO method all of the lower cost brought forward from the previous period is charged as an expense against the current period. The closing stock is derived only from current period costs. With the AVECO method the opening stock is merged with the units produced in the current period and is thus allocated between cost of sales and closing stocks. Therefore some of the lower cost brought forward from the previous period is incorporated in the closing stock at the end of the period.

Cost–volume–profit analysis

Solutions to Chapter 9 questions

Question 9.1 Contribution/sales (%) = (0.33 × 40% Aye) + (0.33 × 50% Bee) + (0.33 × ? Cee) = 48%
Cee = 54% (Balancing figure)
The total contribution/sales ratio for the revised sales mix is:
(0.40 × 40% Aye) + (0.25 × 50% Bee) + (0.35 × 54% Cee) = 47.4%

Answer = C

Question 9.2

Sales	100	110 (100 + 10%)
Variable cost	60	60
Contribution	40	50
Increase = 25%		

Answer = D

Question 9.3 Contribution per unit = 40% × £20 = £8

$$\text{Break-even point} = \frac{\text{Fixed costs (£60 000)}}{\text{Contribution per unit (£8)}} = 7500 \text{ units}$$

Answer = E

Change in activity = 2350 m^2
Change in costs = £9635
Variable cost per metre = £4.10 (£9635/2350)
Fixed costs at 15 100 m^2 = £21 675 (£83 585 − (15 100 × £4.10))
Total cost at 16 200 m^2 = £88 095 (£21 675 + (16 200 × £4.10))

Answer = A

Contribution = Net profit (£56 400) + Fixed costs (£30 000) = £86 400
Contribution/Sales ratio = 0.3
Sales = £86 400/0.3 = £288 000
Variable costs = 70% of sales = £201 600
Direct wages = 20% of £201 600 = £40 320

Answer = C

Question 9.4

Question 9.5

Question 9.6

The unit cost for direct labour and materials are constant per unit so all of the costs are variable. Production overheads are not constant per unit thus suggesting that they include a fixed element. The production overheads are £20 000 (1000 × £20) at an output of 1000 units and £24 800 (2000 × £12.40) at an output of 2000 units. The increase in overheads of £4800 for an additional output of 1000 units arises from an increase in variable costs. Therefore the production overhead variable cost per unit of output is £4.80. At an output level of 1000 units total production variable costs are £4800 so the fixed costs are £15 200 (£20 000 − £4800). Hence, total unit variable cost is £4.80 + £8 + £7 = £19.80.

Answer = E

Question 9.7

(a) (i) Total sales revenue line showing total sales revenues at each level of activity.
     (ii) Total cost line for each level of activity.
     (iii) Total variable cost line for each level of activity.
     (iv) Break-even point in sales revenues.
     (v) Break-even point (units of activity).
     (vi) The difference between the lines represents the total fixed costs for the period.
     Note that the diagram shown in the question is a contribution break-even chart.

(b) See 'Cost–volume–profit analysis assumptions' in Chapter 9 for the answer to this question.

(c) The answer to this question should explain why it is important to adopt a flexible budget approach when applying the controllability principle to control costs. For an explanation of why flexible budgets are required see section titled 'Dealing with the distorting effects of uncontrollable factors after the measurement period' in Chapter 14. The answer should also emphasize that cost behaviour should be thoroughly understood in order to apply the principle of flexible budgeting. In particular, an analysis of costs into their fixed and variable elements is required.

Question 9.11

(a) See Figure Q9.11.

(b) See Chapter 9 for the answer to this question.

(c) The major limitations are:
     (i) Costs and revenue may only be linear within a certain output range.
     (ii) In practice, it is difficult to separate fixed and variable costs, and the calculations will represent an approximation.
     (iii) It is assumed that profits are calculated on a variable costing basis.
     (iv) Analysis assumes a single product is sold or a constant sales mix is maintained.

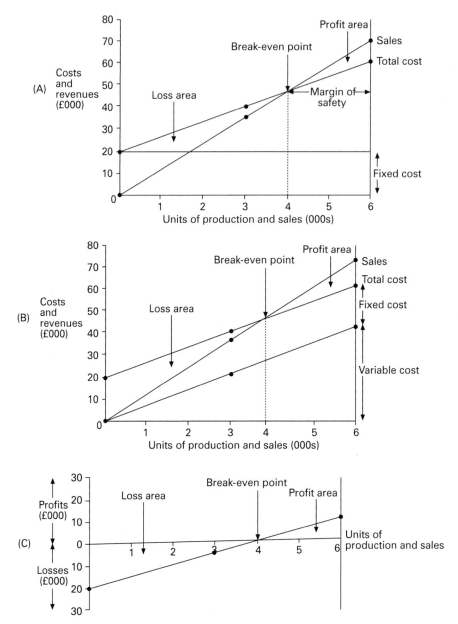

Figures Q9.11 *(A) Break-even chart. (B) Contribution graph. (C) Profit–volume graph.*

(d) The advantages are:
  (i) The information can be absorbed at a glance without the need for detailed figures.
  (ii) Essential features are emphasized.
  (iii) The graphical presentation can be easily understood by non-accountants.

Question 9.12 (a) This question requires the separation of total cost into the fixed and variable elements using the high–low method.

	Low (£)		High (£)	
Sales at £30 000 per unit	480 000	(16 × £30 000)	900 000	(30 × £30 000)
Profit	40 000		250 000	
Total costs (difference)	440 000		650 000	

An increase in output of 14 units results in an increase in total costs of £210 000. Assuming that fixed costs are constant for all activity levels the variable cost per unit is £15 000 (£210 000/14 units). At 30 units activity the variable costs will be £450 000 and monthly fixed costs are £200 000 (£650 000 − £450 000). Over a six-month period total fixed costs are £1 200 000.

$$\text{Break-even point} = \text{Fixed costs (£1 200 000)/unit contribution (£15 000)}$$
$$= 80 \text{ units}$$

See Figure Q9.12 for graph.

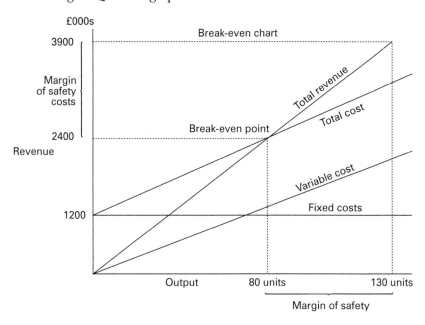

Figure Q9.12

(b) Revised unit
    contribution   £10 000
    Revised total
    contribution   £143 000 (130 units × £1.10 × £10 000)
    Revised profit   £230 000 (£1 430 000 − £1 200 000 fixed costs)
    Current profit   £750 000 (130 × £15 000 − £1 200 000 fixed costs)

The selling price should not be reduced because profits will decline by £520 000.

(c) Costs may not be variable and fixed throughout the entire production range. For example, unit variable cost may not be constant because of bulk discounts on purchases and increasing and decreasing returns (see 'Economists' model', Chapter 9). Costs may also be semi-fixed or semi-variable (see Chapter 2 for an explanation of these terms).

(a) Break-even point = $\dfrac{\text{fixed costs (£1 212 000)}}{\text{average contribution per £ of sales (£0.505)}}$ = £2 400 000

Question 9.13

Average contribution per £ of sales = [0.7 × (£1 − £0.45)] + [0.3 × (£1 − £0.6)]

(b) The graph (Figure Q9.13) is based on the following calculations:

> Zero activity: loss = £1 212 000 (fixed costs)
> £4 m existing sales: (£4m × £0.505) − £1 212 000 = £808 000 profit
> £4 m revised sales: (£4m × £0.475) − £1 212 000 = £688 000 profit
> Existing break-even point: £2 400 000
> Revised break-even point: £2 551 579 (£1 212 000/£0.475)
> Revised contribution per £ of sales: (0.5 × £0.55) + (0.5 × £0.40) = £0.475

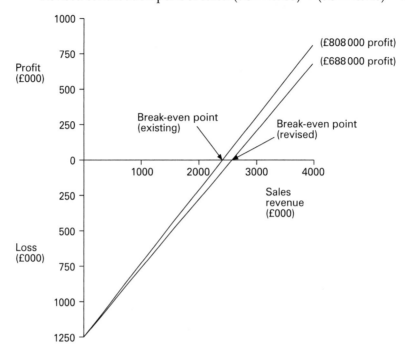

Figure Q9.13 *Profit–volume chart.*

(c) $$\frac{\text{Required contribution}}{\text{Contribution per £ of sales}} = \frac{£455\,000 + £700\,000}{£0.55} = £2\,100\,000$$

Question 9.16

(a) See Figures Q9.16(A) and Q9.16(B) for the break-even charts.

(b) Both charts indicate that each product has three break-even points. With the Standard quality, profits are earned on sales from 80 000 to 99 999 units and above 140 000 units; whereas with the De Luxe quality, profits are earned on sales from 71 429 − 99 999 units and above 114 286 units. The charts therefore provide guidance regarding the level of sales at which to aim.

(c) *Expected unit sales*

> Standard: (172 000 × 0.1) + (160 000 × 0.7) + (148 000 × 0.2) = 158 800
> De Luxe: (195 500 × 0.3) + (156 500 × 0.5) + (109 500 × 0.2) = 158 800

Expected profits

	Standard (£)	De Luxe (£)
Total contribution	397 000 (158 800 × £2.50)	555 800 (158 800 × £3.50)
Fixed costs	350 000	400 000
Profit	47 000	155 800

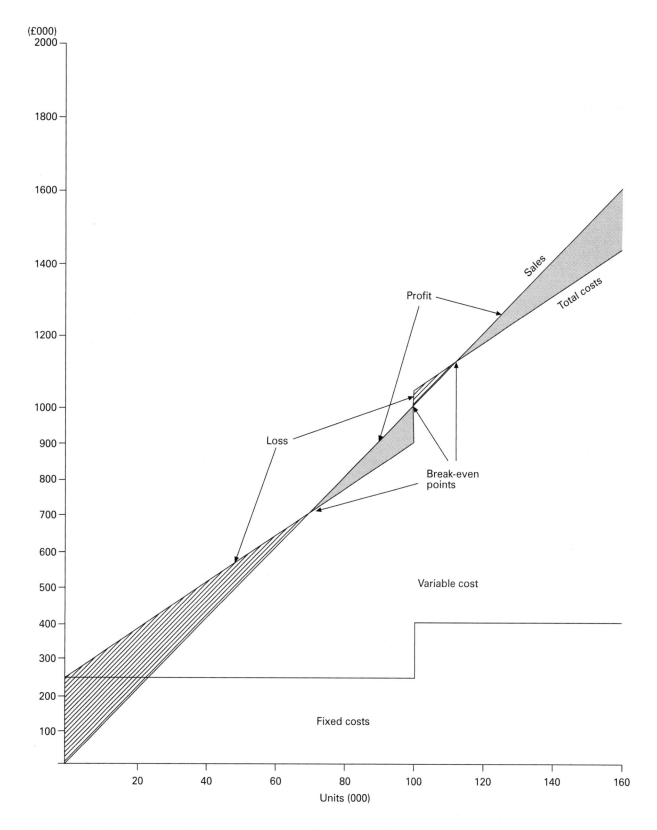

Figure Q9.16 *(A) Break-even chart – Deluxe quality.*

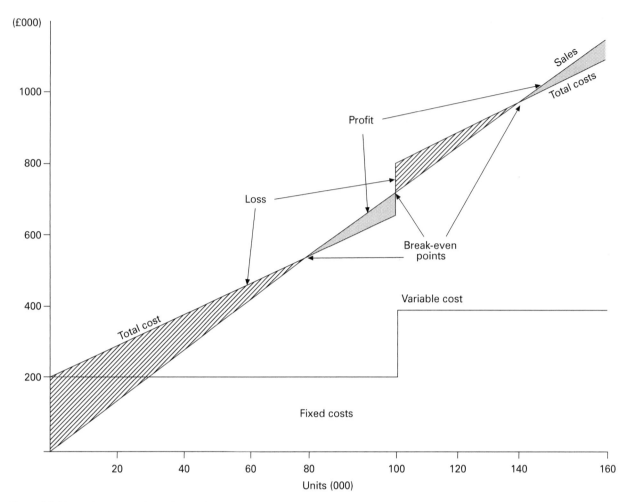

Figure Q9.16 *(B) Break-even chart – Standard quality.*

Margin of safety

Standard: expected sales volume (158 800) − break-even point (140 000)
= 18 800 units

De Luxe: expected sales volume (158 800) − break-even point (114 286)
= 44 514 units

(d) The profit probability distributions for the products are:

| | Standard | | | De Luxe | |
Demand	probability	Profits (£)	Demand	Probability	Profits/(loss) (£)
172 000	0.1	80 000	195 500	0.3	284 250
160 000	0.7	50 000	156 500	0.5	147 750
148 000	0.2	20 000	109 500	0.2	(16 750)

The De Luxe model has the higher expected profit, but is also more risky than the Standard product. There is a 0.2 probability that the De Luxe model will make a loss, whereas there is a zero probability that the Standard product will make a loss. The decision as to which product to produce will depend upon management's attitude towards risk and the future profitability from its other products. If the company is currently making a loss it may be inappropriate to choose the product that could make a loss. On the other hand, the rewards from the De Luxe model are much higher, and, if the company can survive if the worst outcome occurs, there is a strong argument for producing the De Luxe product.

(a) *With promotion*

Unit variable cost	=	£1.54 (55% × £2.80)
Promotional selling price	=	£2.24 (80% × £2.80)
Promotional contribution per unit	=	£0.70
Contribution for 4 week promotion period	=	£16 800 (6000 × 4 weeks × £0.70)
Less incremental fixed costs	=	£5 400
		£11 400

Without promotion

Normal contribution per unit	=	£1.26 (£2.80 × 45%)
Contribution for 4 week period	=	£12 096 (£1.26 × 2400 × 4 weeks)

Therefore the promotion results in a reduction in profits of £696.

(b)
Required contribution	=	£17 496 (£12 096 + £5400 fixed costs)
Required sales volume in units	=	24 994 (£17 496/£0.70 unit contribution)
Required weekly sales volume	=	6249 units (24 994/4 weeks)
Sales multiplier required	=	2.6 (6249/2400)

(c) Other factors to be considered are:
  (i) The effect of the promotion on sales after the promotion period.
  (ii) Impact of the promotion on sales of other products during and after the promotion.

(a) *Calculation of total contribution*

		(£)
Product A (460 000 × £1.80)	=	828 000
Product B (1 000 000 × £0.78)	=	780 000
Product C (380 000 × £1.40)	=	532 000
		2 140 000

Calculation of total sales revenue

		(£)
Product A (460 000 × £3)	=	1 380 000
Product B (1 000 000 × £2.45)	=	2 450 000
Product C (380 000 × £4)	=	1 520 000
		5 350 000

$$\text{Break-even point (sales revenue basis)} = \frac{\text{fixed costs (£1 710 000)} \times \text{total sales (£5 350 000)}}{\text{total contribution (2 140 000)}}$$

$$= £4 275 000$$

(b) *£2.75 selling price*

Total contribution 590 000 × (£2.75 − £1.20)	914 500
Existing planned contribution	828 000
Extra contribution	86 500
Less additional fixed costs	60 000
Additional contribution to general fixed costs	26 500

£2.55 selling price

	(£)
Total contribution 650 000 × (£2.55 − £1.20)	877 500
Existing planned contribution	828 000
Extra contribution	49 500
Less additional fixed costs	60 000
Contribution to general fixed costs	(10 500)

It is worthwhile incurring the expenditure on advertising and sales promotion at a selling price of £2.75.

(c) Required contribution = existing contribution (£828 000)
$\qquad$ + additional fixed costs (£60 000)
$\qquad$ = £888 000

The required sales volume at a selling price of £2.75 that will generate a total contribution of £888 000 is 572 903 units (£888 000/£1.55 unit contribution).

(d) See 'Margin of safety' in Chapter 9 for the answer to this question. At the existing selling price for product A, the margin of safety for Z Ltd is £1 075 000 (£5 350 000 sales revenue − £4 275 000 break-even point) of sales revenue. This is 20.1% of the current level of sales. If Z Ltd incurs the advertising and promotion expenditure and reduces the selling price to £2.75 for product A, the break-even point will increase to £4 446 000 and total sales revenue will increase to £5 593 000. This will result in a margin of safety of £1 147 000 or 20.5% of sales.

Question 9.22 (a) (i)

Products	1	2	3	Total
1. Unit contribution	£1.31	£0.63	£1.87	
2. Specific fixed costs per unit	£0.49	£0.35	£0.62	
3. General fixed costs per unit	£0.46	£0.46	£0.46	
4. Sales volume (000s units)	98.2	42.1	111.8	252.1
5. Total contribution (1 × 4)	£128.642	£26.523	£209.066	£364.231
6. Total specific fixed costs (2 × 4)	£48.118	£14.735	£69.316	£132.169
7. Total general fixed costs (3 × 4)	£45.172	£19.366	£51.428	£115.966
8. Unit selling price	£2.92	£1.35	£2.83	
9. Total sales revenue (8 × 4)	£286.744	£56.835	£316.394	£659.973

Average contribution per unit = Total contribution (£364.231)/sales volume
$\qquad$ (252.1)
$\qquad$ = £1.4448

Average selling price per unit = Total sales revenue (£659.973)/sales
$\qquad$ volume (252.1)
$\qquad$ = £2.6179

$$\text{Break-even point (units)} = \frac{\text{Total fixed costs}}{\text{Average contribution per unit}}$$

$\qquad$ = (£132.169 + £115.966)/£1.4448
$\qquad$ = 171.743 units

Break-even point (sales value) = 171.743 units × average selling price
$\qquad$ (£2.6179)
$\qquad$ = £449.606

Alternatively, the break-even point (sales value) can be calculated using the following formula:

$$\text{Break-even point} = \frac{\text{Fixed costs (£132.169 + £115.966)}}{\text{Total contribution (£364.231)}} \times \text{Total sales (£659.973)}$$

$\qquad$ = £449.606

It is assumed that the question requires the calculation of the break-even point to cover both general and specific fixed costs. An alternative answer would have been to present details of the break-even point to cover only specific fixed costs.

(ii) The planned sales mix for Product 2 that was used to calculate the break-even point in (i) is 42.1/252.1. Therefore the number of units of Product 2 at the break-even point is:

$$42.1/252.1 \times 171\ 743 \text{ units} = 28\ 681$$

(b) At the forecast sales volume the profit/contributions are as follows:

	(£000s)
Contributions to all fixed costs	26.523
Less specific fixed costs	14.735
Contribution to general fixed costs	11.788
Less share of general fixed costs	19.366
Net loss	7.578

Product 2 provides a contribution of £11 788 towards general fixed costs and, unless savings in general fixed costs in excess of £11 788 can be made if Product 2 is abandoned, it is still viable to produce Product 2. If the company ceases production of Product 2 it will lose a contribution of £11 788 and total profits will decline by £11 788. The company should investigate whether a greater contribution than £11 788 can be generated from the resources. If this is not possible the company should continue production of Product 2.

Question 9.23

	Product A		Product B		Product C	
	£/unit	% of sales	£/unit	% of sales	£/unit	% of sales
Sales[a]	1.560	100.0	1.700	100.0	1.250	100.0
Variable production cost[b]	0.780	50.0	1.000	58.8	0.500	40.0
Variable non-production cost[c]	0.156	10.0	0.170	10.0	0.125	10.0
Total variable cost	0.936	60.0	1.170	68.8	0.625	50.0
Contribution	0.624	40.0	0.530	31.2	0.625	50.0

Notes
[a] Total sales revenue/units sold (Product A = £1 794 000/1 150 000 units = £1.56).
[b] Production cost of sales/units sold – £0.30 fixed overheads.
[c] 10% of selling price.

(b)

	A	B	C	Total
(1) Units sold	1150	2200	2360	5710
(2) Sales mix[a]	20.14%	38.53%	41.33%	
(3) Unit contribution from (a)	£0.624	£0.530	£0.625	
(4) Total contribution (1 × 3)	£717.6	£1166	£1475	3358.6
(5) Sales revenues	1794	3740	2950	

Note
[a] Product A = 1150 units/5710 units, B = 2200/5710, C = 2360/5710

Average contribution per unit sold = £3358.6/5710 units = £0.5882

Total units sold to generate a contribution of £3.75m = £3.75m/£0.5882
$$= 6\ 375\ 383 \text{ units}$$

Total sales of 6 375 383 units at the current sales mix is:

Product A = 20.14% × 6 375 383 units = 1 284 002 units
         B = 38.53% × 6 375 383 units = 2 456 435 units
         C = 41.33% × 6 375 383 units = 2 634 946 units

Answer in sales revenues:

Product A = 1 284 002 units × £1.560 unit selling price = £2 003 043
         B = 2 456 435 units × £1.70 unit selling price   = £4 175 940
         C = 2 634 946 units × £1.25 unit selling price   = £3 293 683
         Total sales   £9 472 663

Question 9.25

Task 1

	(£)	(£)
Sales		2 106 000
Less variable cost of sales:		
Cost of beds	1 620 000	
Commission	210 600	
Transport	216 000	2 046 600
Contribution		59 400

Average contribution per bed sold = £59 400/5400   = £11
Fixed costs (£8450 + £10 000 + £40 000 + £40 000) = £98 450

$$\text{Break-even point (units)} = \frac{\text{Fixed costs (£98 450)}}{\text{Contribution per unit (£11)}} = 8950 \text{ beds}$$

Average selling price per unit (£2 106 000/5400 beds)   = £390
Break-even point (sales revenue) = 8950 beds at £390   = £3 490 500

Task 2

The letter should include the items listed in (a) to (e) below:

(a) Required contribution: (£)
    Salary   36 550
    Interest lost   15 000
    Fixed costs shown in Task 1   98 450
                                                150 000
    Less manager's salary saved   40 000
    Total contribution   110 000

The minimum profit required to compensate for loss of salary and interest is £11 550 (£110 000 − £98 450 fixed costs).

(b) Required volume = Required contribution (£110 000)/Contribution per unit (£11)
    = 10 000 beds

(c) Average life of a bed = (9 years × 0.10) + (10 years × 0.60) + (11 years × 0.3) = 10.2 years

Total bed population = 44 880 households × 2.1 beds per market = 94 248

$$\text{Estimated annual demand} = \frac{94\,248 \text{ beds}}{\text{Average replacement period (10.2 years)}}$$
$$= 9\,240 \text{ beds}$$

(d) The proposal will not achieve the desired profit. Estimated annual sales are 9240 beds but 10 000 beds must be sold to achieve the desired profit. The shortfall of 760 beds will result in profit being £8360 (760 × £11) less than the desired profit.

(e) The estimate of maximum annual sales volume may prove to be inaccurate because of the following reasons:
   (i) The population of Mytown may differ from the sample population. For example the population of Mytown might contain a greater proportion of elderly people or younger people with families. Either of these situations may result in the buying habits of the population of Mytown being different from the sample proportion.
   (ii) The data is historic and does not take into account future changes such as an increase in wealth of the population, change in composition or a change in buying habits arising from different types of beds being marketed.

Task 3

This question requires a knowledge of the material covered in Chapter 10. Therefore you should delay attempting this question until you have understood the content of Chapter 11.

	A (£)	B (£)	C (£)	Total
Selling price	240	448	672	
Unit purchase cost	130	310	550	
Carriage inwards	20	20	20	
Contribution	90	118	102	
Square metres per bed	3	4	5	
Contribution per square metre	£30	£29.50	£20.40	
Ranking	1	2	3	
Maximum demand	35	45	20	
Storage required (square metres)	105	180	100	385

Monthly sales schedule and statement of profitability:

	(£)	(£)
Contribution from sales of A (35 × £90)		3150
Contribution from sales of B (45 × £118)		5310
Contribution from sales of C (3^a × £102)		306
		8766
Less specific avoidable fixed costs:		
Staff costs	3780	
Departmental fixed overheads	2000	5780
Contribution to general fixed overheads		2986
Less general fixed overheads		2520
Departmental profit		466

Note:
[a] The balance of storage space available for Model C is 300 square metres less the amount allocated to A and B (285 metres) = 15 metres. This will result in the sales of 3 beds (15 metres/5 metres per bed).

(a)

Question 9.27

		(£000)
Period 2 sales volume at period 1 prices (1108.1 × 100/105)	=	1055.333
Period 1 sales volume at period 1 prices	=	902.000
Increase in sales attributable to sales volume		153.333
% increase in sales volume (153.333/902 × 100)	=	17%

(b) (i)

	(£000)
Increase in sales attributable to sales volume	153.333
Contribution based on period 1 cost structure (60% of sales)	92.000
Fixed costs are assumed to be unaffected by volume changes	
Increase in profit attributable to volume	92.000

(b) (ii)

	Period 2 sales volume at period 1 prices and period 1 production methods (£000)	Period 2 sales volume at period 1 prices and period 2 production methods (£000)
Sales	1055.333	1055.333
Variable costs	422.133[a]	379.905[b]
Contribution	633.200	675.428
Fixed costs	490.500[c]	522.857[d]
Net profit	142.700	152.571

	(£000)
Reduction in variable costs arising from reorganization in production methods	42.228
Increase in fixed costs arising from reorganization in production methods	(32.357)
	9.871

Notes:
[a] Sales × period 1 contribution to sales ratio of 60%
[b] £398.9 × 100/105
[c] Fixed costs are assumed to be unaffected by changes in sales volume
[d] £549.0 × 100/105

(c) Required contribution = Period 2 fixed costs (£549 000) + Period 1 profit (£50 700) = £599,700. The contribution/sales ratio (profit–volume ratio) for period 2 is 64% (£709.2/£1108.1). In other words each £1 sale generates £0.64 contribution. To generate a contribution of £599 700 sales revenue of £937 031 is required (£599 700/0.64).

(d) The formula for the break-even point in sales revenue is:

$$\left[\frac{\text{Fixed costs}}{\text{Contribution/sales ratio}} \text{ or Fixed costs} \times \frac{\text{Sales}}{\text{Contribution}} \right]$$

When sales revenue generates a contribution that is exactly equal to fixed costs break-even point is achieved. To determine this level of sales revenue fixed costs must be divided by the rate at which contribution is made per £1 of sales.

Question 9.28 (a) *Analysis of semi-variable costs[a]*

Method A: variable element = $\dfrac{\text{increase in costs}}{\text{increase in activity}} = \dfrac{£10\,000}{100\,000 \text{ copies}}$

= £0.10 per copy

fixed element = total semi-variable cost (£55 000) − variable cost (£35 000) at an activity level of 350 000 copies

Therefore fixed element = £20 000

Method B: variable element = $\dfrac{\text{increase in costs}}{\text{increase in activity}} = \dfrac{£5000}{100\,000 \text{ copies}}$

= £0.05 per copy

fixed element = total semi-variable cost (£47 500) − variable costs (£17 500) at an activity level of 350 000 copies

Therefore fixed element = £30 000

Note
[a]The analysis is based on a comparison of total costs and activity levels at 350 000 and 450 000 copies per year.

Contribution per copy of new magazine

	Method A (£)	Method B (£)
Selling price	1.00	1.00
Variable cost (given)	(0.55)	(0.50)
Variable element of semi-variable cost	(0.10)	(0.05)
Lost contribution from existing magazine	(0.05)	(0.05)
Contribution	0.30	0.40

Calculation of net increase in company profits

	Method A			Method B		
Copies sold	500 000	400 000	600 000	500 000	400 000	600 000
Contribution per copy	£0.30	£0.30	£0.30	£0.40	£0.40	£0.40
Total contribution	£150 000	£120 000	£180 000	£200 000	£160 000	£240 000
Fixed costs[a]	£100 000	£100 000	£100 000	£150 000	£150 000	£150 000
Net increase in profit	£50 000	£20 000	£80 000	£50 000	£10 000	£90 000

Note
[a]Method A = specific fixed costs (£80 000) + semi-variable element (£20 000)
= £100 000
Method B = specific fixed costs (£120 000) + semi-variable element (£30 000)
= £150 000

(b)
$$\text{Break-even point} = \frac{\text{fixed costs}}{\text{contribution per unit}}$$

Method A = £100 000/0.30 = 333 333 copies
Method B = £150 000/0.40 = 375 000 copies

The margin of safety is the difference between the anticipated sales and the break-even point sales:

Method A = 500 000 − 333 333 = 166 667 copies
Method B = 500 000 − 375 000 = 125 000 copies

(c) Method B has a higher break-even point and a higher contribution per copy sold. This implies that profits from Method B are more vulnerable to a decline in sales volume. However, higher profits are obtained with Method B when sales are high (see 600 000 copies in (B)).

The break-even point from the sale of the existing magazine is 160 000 copies (£80 000/£0.50) and the current level of monthly sales is 220 000 copies. Therefore sales can drop by 60 000 copies before break-even point is reached. For every 10 copies sold of the new publication, sales of the existing publication will be reduced by one copy. Consequently, if more than 600 000 copies of the new publication are sold, the existing magazine will make a loss. If sales of the new magazine are expected to consistently exceed 600 000 copies then the viability of the existing magazine must be questioned.

Question 9.29

(a) (i) The opportunity costs of producing cassettes are the salary forgone of £1000 per month and the rental forgone of £400 per month.
(ii) The consultant's fees and development costs represent sunk costs.

(b) The following information can be obtained from the report.

	£10 selling price	£9 selling price
Sales quantity	7500–10 000 units	12 000–18 000 units
Fixed costs[a]	£13 525	£17 525
Profit at maximum sales[b]	£3 975	£4 975
Profit/(loss) at minimum sales[c]	(£400)	(£2 525)
Break-even point[d]	7 729 units	14 020 units
Margin of safety:		
Below maximum	2 271 units	3 980 units
Above minimum	229 units	2 020 units

Notes
[a] Fixed production cost + £1400 opportunity cost
[b] (10 000 units × £1.75 contribution) − £13 525 fixed costs = £3975 profit
   (18 000 units × £1.25 contribution) − £17 525 fixed costs = £4975 profit
[c] (7 500 units × £1.75 contribution) − £13 525 fixed costs = £400 loss
   (12 000 units × £1.25 contribution) − £17 525 fixed costs = £2525 loss
[d] Fixed costs/contribution per unit

Conclusions
  (i) The £10 selling price is less risky than the £9 selling price. With the £10 selling price, the maximum loss is lower and the break-even point is only 3% above minimum sales (compared with 17% for a £9 selling price).
 (ii) The £9 selling price will yield the higher profits if maximum sales quantity is achieved.
(iii) In order to earn £3975 profits at a £9 selling price, we must sell 17 200 units (required contribution of 17 525 fixed costs plus £3975 divided by a contribution per unit of £1.25).

Additional information required
  (i) Details of capital employed for each selling price.
 (ii) Details of additional finance required to finance the working capital and the relevant interest cost so as to determine the cost of financing the working capital.
(iii) Estimated probability of units sold at different selling prices.
(iv) How long will the project remain viable?
 (v) Details of range of possible costs. Are the cost figures given in the question certain?

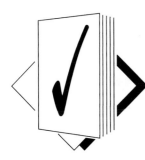

Measuring relevant costs and revenues for decision-making

Solutions to Chapter 10 questions

Question summary

Because the materials are readily available the decision to use them on the special **Question 10.1**
order will not result in any reduced output of product F. Thus no opportunity cost
will be involved. The company can sell Material R for £2.60 but since they are used
regularly it will be necessary to replace them at £3. This would be an unprofitable
course of action. The decision to use the materials on the special order will necessitate
their replacement. Therefore the relevant cost of materials is the replacement cost of
£3 per kg. The total relevant cost of the order for materials is £2400 (800 kg × £3).

Answer = C

The shadow price is the opportunity cost or contribution per unit of a scarce resource. **Question 10.2**

	Quone	Qutwo
Contribution per unit	£8	£8.50
Kg per unit	3 (£6/£2)	2.50 (£5/£2)
Contribution per kg	£2.67	£3.40

Scarce materials will be used to make Qutwos and will yield a contribution of £3.40
per kg. Therefore the opportunity cost is £3.40 per kg.

Answer = D

Question 10.3 (a) General fixed overheads are recovered at a rate of 80% of direct labour cost (£1.20/£1.50). Therefore general fixed overheads for Product M2 are £0.80 (80% × £1 Direct Labour Cost). The balance of £0.20 represents specific fixed costs for Product M2. The incremental costs of manufacturing are:

	Product M1	Product M2
	(£)	(£)
Direct costs	4.60	4.40
Specified fixed costs		0.20
Maximum purchase price	4.60	4.60

Answer = B

(b) General fixed overheads = £12 000 allocated to M1 (10 000 × £1.20)
= £10 000 allocated to M2 (12 500 × £1 less
£2 500 specific fixed costs)
£22 000

$$\text{Number of units to be sold} = \frac{\text{Fixed costs (£22 000)} + \text{Desired profit (£50 000)}}{\text{Unit contribution (£5.40)}}$$

= 13 333 units

Answer = C

Question 10.4 (a)

	(£)
Purchase price of component from supplier	50
Additional cost of manufacturing (variable cost only)	34
Saving if component manufactured	16

The component should be manufactured provided the following assumptions are correct:

(i) Direct labour represents the *additional* labour cost of producing the component.

(ii) The company will not incur any additional fixed overheads if the component is manufactured.

(iii) There are no scarce resources. Therefore the manufacture of the component will not restrict the production of other more profitable products.

(b) (i) Additional fixed costs of £56 000 will be incurred, but there will be a saving in purchasing costs of £16 per unit produced. The break-even point is 3500 units (fixed costs of £56 000/£16 per unit saving). If the quantity of components manufactured per year is less than 3500 units then it will be cheaper to purchase from the outside supplier.

(ii) The contribution per unit sold from the existing product is £40 and each unit produced uses 8 scarce labour hours. The contribution per labour hour is £5. Therefore if the component is manufactured, 4 scarce labour hours will be used, resulting in a lost contribution of £20. Hence the relevant cost of manufacturing the components is £54, consisting of £34 incremental cost plus a lost contribution of £20. The component should be purchased from the supplier.

(c) The book value of the equipment is a sunk cost and is not relevant to the decision whether the company should purchase or continue to manufacture the components. If we cease production now, the written-down value will be written off in a lump sum, whereas if we continue production, the written-down value will be written off over a period of years. Future cash outflows on the equipment will not be affected by the decision to purchase or continue to manufacture the components. For an illustration of the irrelevance of the written down value of assets for decision-making purposes see 'Replacement of equipment' in Chapter 10.

(a)

	North East (£)	South coast (£)
Material X from stock (1)	19 440	
Material Y from stock (2)		49 600
Firm orders of material X (3)	27 360	
Material X not yet ordered (4)	60 000	
Material Z not yet ordered (5)		71 200
Labour (6)	86 000	110 000
Site management (7)	—	—
Staff accommodation and travel for site management (8)	6 800	5 600
Plant rental received (9)	(6 000)	—
Penalty clause (10)		28 000
	193 600	264 400
Contract price	288 000	352 000
Net benefit	94 400	87 600

(b) (i) If material X is not used on the North East contract the most beneficial use is to use it as a substitute material thus avoiding future purchases of £19 440 (0.9 × 21 600). Therefore by using the stock quantity of material X the company will have to spend £19 440 on the other materials.

(ii) Material Y is in common use and the company should not dispose of it. Using the materials on the South coast contract will mean that they will have to be replaced at a cost of £49 600 (£24 800 × 2). Therefore the future cash flow impact of taking on the contract is £49 600.

(iii) It is assumed that with firm orders for materials it is not possible to cancel the purchase. Therefore the cost will occur whatever future alternative is selected. The materials will be used as a substitute material if they are not used on the contract and therefore, based on the same reasoning as note 1 above, the relevant cost is the purchase price of the substitute material (0.9 × £30 400).

(iv) The material has not been ordered and the cost will only be incurred if the contract is undertaken. Therefore additional cash flows of £60 000 will be incurred if the company takes on the North East contract.

(v) The same principles apply here as were explained in point 4 and additional cash flows of £71 200 will be incurred only if the company takes on the South coast contract.

(vi) It is assumed that labour is an incremental cost and therefore relevant.

(vii) The site management function is performed by staff at central headquarters. It is assumed that the total company costs in respect of site management will remain unchanged in the short term whatever contracts are taken on. Site management costs are therefore irrelevant.

(viii) The costs would be undertaken only if the contracts are undertaken. Therefore they are relevant costs.

(ix) If the North East contract is undertaken the company will be able to hire out surplus plant and obtain a £6000 cash inflow.

(x) If the South coast contract is undertaken the company will have to withdraw from the North East contract and incur a penalty cost of £28 000.

(xi) The headquarter costs will continue whichever alternative is selected and they are not relevant costs.

(xii) It is assumed that there will be no differential cash flows relating to notional interest. However, if the interest costs associated with the contract differ then they would be relevant and should be included in the analysis.

(xiii) Depreciation is a sunk cost and irrelevant for decision-making.

Question 10.9 (a) *Calculation of minimum selling price:*

	(£)
Direct materials: Steel[a]	55.00
Brass Fittings[b]	20.00
Direct Labour: Skilled[c]	300.00
Semi-skilled[d]	—
Overhead[e]	7.50
Estimating time[f]	—
Administration[g]	—
Relevant cost of the order	382.50

Notes:

[a] Using the materials for the order will result in them having to be replaced. Therefore future cash outflows will increase by £55.

[b] Future cash outflows of £20 will be incurred.

[c] The required labour hours can be obtained by reducing production of another product involving a lost contribution before deducting the labour cost of £21 (£13 + £8) per hour (note that the labour cost will be incurred for all alternatives and therefore is not an incremental cash flow). Alternatively, the company can pay additional wages involving overtime of £300 (25 hours × £12). Therefore the latter course of action is the most economical and the incremental cash flows from undertaking the order will be £300.

[d] No incremental cost is involved since the alternative is paid idle time.

[e] The only incremental cost is power consisting of 10 hours at £0.75 per hour.

[f] Estimating time is a sunk cost.

[g] Administration does not involve any incremental cash flows.

(b) Factors to be considered include:
   (i) time period for repeat orders, the number of repeat orders and the likely demand;
   (ii) the cash flows generated from the alternative use of the capacity;
   (iii) competition to obtain future orders from Exe plc;
   (iv) estimated price quotations from competitors.

(c) *Limiting factor presentation:*

	Product X	Product Y
Product contribution	£10	£20
Kg of material used per product	1	4
Contribution per kg	£10	£5

Thus scarce materials should be allocated to Product X since it yields a contribution of £5 per kg in excess of the contribution derived from Product Y.

Opportunity cost approach:

	Product X	Product Y
Product contribution at acquisition cost	£10	£20
Lost contribution from alternative use:		
1 kg allocated to Y at £5 per kg	(£5)	
4 kg allocated to X at £10 per kg		£40
Cash flow impact per product	+£5	−£20
Cash flow impact per kg	+£5 (£5/1 kg)	−£5 (£20/4 kg)

The above analysis shows that X yields a contribution of £5 per kg when taking alternative uses of the materials into consideration. Producing Product Y results in the contribution being reduced by £5 per kg taking into account the alternative use of the materials. This is consistent with the limiting factor approach which indicates that the company is £5 per kg better off using the materials for X or £5 per kg worse off from using the materials for Y.

(a) (i)

	Product I (£000)	Product II (£000)	Product III (£000)	Total (£000)
Sales	2475	3948	1520	7943
Contribution	1170	1692	532	3394
Attributable fixed costs	(275)	(337)	(296)	(908)
General fixed costs[a]	(520)	(829)	(319)	(1668)
	(795)	(1166)	(615)	(2576)
Profit	375	526	(83)	818
	= £1.6/unit	= £1.40/unit	= (£0.04/unit)	

Note
[a]General fixed costs are allocated to products at 21% of total sales revenue (£1668/£7943).

(ii) If Product III is discontinued it is assumed that variable costs and attributable (i.e. specific) fixed costs are avoidable. It is assumed that general fixed costs are common and unavoidable to all products and will remain unchanged if Product III is discontinued. However, it is possible that some general fixed costs may be avoidable in the longer term. The revised profits if Product III is discontinued will be:

	(£000s)
Contribution of Products I and II (£1170 + £1692)	2862
Attributable fixed costs (£275 + £337)	(612)
General fixed costs	(1668)
Profit	582

Profits will decline by £236 000 (£818 − £582) if Product III is discontinued because A Ltd will no longer obtain a contribution of £236 000 (£532 − £296) towards general fixed costs.

(iii) Extra sales of 15 385 units (£80 000 additional fixed costs/£5.20 unit contribution) will be required to cover the additional advertising expenditure. It is assumed that existing fixed costs will remain unchanged.

(iv) The revised unit contribution will be £3.45 (£9.45 − £6).

$$\text{Required sales} = \frac{\text{£1 692 000 (existing total contribution)}}{\text{£3.45 revised unit contribution}}$$

= 490 435 units (an increase of 30.4% over the budgeted sales of 376 000 units)

(b) The following factors will influence cost behaviour in response to changes in activity:
   (i) The magnitude of the change in activity (more costs are likely to be affected when there is a large change in activity).
   (ii) Type of expense (some expenses are directly variable with volume such as direct materials, whereas others are fixed or semi-fixed).
   (iii) Management policy (some expenses are varied at the discretion of management, e.g. advertising).
   (iv) The time period (in the long term, all costs can be changed in response to changes in activity whereas in the short term, some costs, e.g. salaries of supervisors, will remain unchanged).

Question 10.11 (a) Company gross profit % = 38% (£3268/£8600 × 100)

Therefore Division 5 gross profit % = 19%
Division 5 sales = £860 000 (10% × £8.6m)
Division 5 gross profit = £163 400 (19% × £860 000)
Division 5 contribution = £479 400 (£316 000 + £163 400)

The situation for the year ahead if the division were not sold would be as follows:

Contribution = £527 340 (£479 400 × 1.1)
Less avoidable fixed costs = £455 700 [£316 000 + (£156 000 − £38 000)] × 1.05
Add contribution from other divisions = £20 000
Expected profit = £91 640

If Division 5 were sold, the capital sum would yield a return of £75 400. Therefore the decision on the basis of the above information should be not to sell Division 5.

(b) Other factors that should influence the decision include:
 (i) The need to focus on a longer-term time horizon. A decision based solely on the year ahead is too short and ignores the long-term impact from selling Division 5.
 (ii) The impact on the morale of the staff working in other divisions arising from the contraction of activities and the potential threat of redundancies.
 (iii) Alternative use of the resources currently deployed in Division 5 instead of their current use.

(c) If Division 5 is sold, the capital sum would yield a return of £75 000, but a contribution of £20 000 is lost. Consequently, a profit of £55 000 is required. The required contribution is therefore £510 700 (£55 000 + £455 700) and the percentage increase required is 6.5% (£510 700/£479 400 − 100%).

Question 10.13 (a)

Planned/total contribution and profit for the year ending 31 December

Route	W (£)	X (£)	Y (£)	Z (£)	Total (£)
Income:					
Adult	140 400	187 200	351 000	137 280	
Child[a]	46 800	74 880	35 100	34 320	
Total	187 200	262 080	386 100	171 600	
Variable costs:					
Fuel and repairs[b]	24 570	21 060	25 740	22 230	
Bus contribution	162 630	241 020	360 360	149 370	
Specific fixed costs:					
Wages[c]	74 880	74 880	74 880	74 880	
Vehicle fixed costs	4 000	4 000	4 000	4 000	
Route contribution	83 750	162 140	281 480	70 490	597 860
General administration					300 000
Profit					297 860

Notes
[a] 52 weeks × 6 days × 5 journeys per day × number of passengers × return fare × 2 vehicles
[b] 52 weeks × 6 days × 5 journeys per day × return travel distance × £0.1875 × 2 vehicles
[c] 52 weeks × 6 days × £120 × 2 vehicles

(b) (i) The relevant (differential) items are the return fares and the average number of passengers per journey:

	Adult (£)	Child (£)
Existing revenue per journey	45 (15 × £3.00)	15 (10 × £1.50)
Revised revenue per journey	45 (12 × £3.75)	12 (8 × £1.50)
Net gain/(loss)	nil	(3)

The contribution per return journey will decrease by £3.

(b) (ii) The above analysis suggests that the fare should not be amended on route W. The only justification is that the current prices result in the average number of passengers being 25 per journey so it is possible that occasionally demand may exceed full capacity of 30 passengers resulting in some passengers not being able to be carried. With the price increase the average number of passengers will be 20 and it is less likely that some passengers will not be able to be carried.

(c) (i)

Annual cost of existing maintenance function

	(£)	(£)
Staffing		
Fitters (£15 808 × 2)	31 616	
Supervisor	24 000	55 616
Material costs		
Bus servicing (499 200 km^a/4000) × £100	12 480	
Bus safety checks (48 per year at £75)	3 600	
Taxi servicing (128 000 km/4000 × 6 vehicles) × £100	19 200	
Taxi safety checks (36 per year at £75)	2 700	37 980
Total cost		93 596

Note
^{a} 160 km per journey × 5 journeys × 52 weeks × 6 days × 2 vehicles

(c) (ii)

	(£)	(£)
Annual cost of keeping own maintenance		
Annual operating costs	93 596	
Cost of new employee	20 000	113 596
Annual cost of buying in maintenance		
Contract cost	90 000	
Redundancy costs for fitters	15 808	105 808
Savings in the first year from buying in maintenance		7 788

There will be a saving after the first year from buying in maintenance of £23 596 because the redundancy cost will be incurred for one year only.

(c) (iii) AZ will lose control of the operations if the service is carried out externally. It will be more difficult to ensure quality of work and schedule the servicing as required. Once the skills have been lost from outsourcing it may be difficult to re-establish them. Also AZ will be at the mercy of the supplier when the contract is re-negotiated. The extent to which AZ will be dependent on the supplier will be influenced by how competitive the market is for providing a maintenance service.

AZ could also consider making vehicle servicing a profit centre which competes with external competitors for the work of the group.

Question 10.14 (a) *Hours of installation labour required to satisfy maximum demand*

		(hours)
Day scan:	2000 units × 3 hours per unit	6 000
Night scan:	3000 units × 4 hours per unit	12 000
Omni scan:	1800 units × 5.5 hours per unit	9 900
		27 900
Available hours		25 000
Shortfall		2 900

Note that the labour hours per unit = installation labour cost/£8.

(b)

	Day scan (£)	Night scan (£)	Omni scan (£)
Selling price	250	320	460
Variable costs			
Material	(70)	(110)	(155)
Manufacturing labour	(40)	(55)	(70)
Installation labour	(24)	(32)	(44)
Variable overheads	(16)	(20)	(28)
Contribution per unit	100	103	163
Installation hours required	3	4	5.5
Contribution per installation hour	£33.33	£25.75	£29.64
Production priority	1st	3rd	2nd

Best production plan

	Units		Hours used
Day scan to maximum demand	2000	(× 3)	6000
Omni scan to maximum demand	1800	(× 5.5)	9900

This leaves (25 000 – 6000 – 9900) = 9100 installation labour hours for Night scan.

Therefore production of Night scan $= \dfrac{9100}{4} = 2275$ units

(c) *Maximum profit achievable*

	Total	Day scan	Omni scan	Night scan
Units		2000	1800	2275
	(£)	(£)	(£)	(£)
Contribution	727 725	200 000	293 400	234 325
Fixed costs	(450 000)			
	277 725			

(d) *Revised contributions*

	Day scan (£ per unit)	Night scan (£ per unit)	Omni scan (£ per unit)
Previous contribution	100	103	163
Reduction[a]	(12)	(16)	(22)
New contribution	88	87	141

Note
[a] Increase in labour cost at £4 per hour.

The profit arising from the production and sales of the maximum demand will be as follows:

	Total	Day scan	Night scan	Omni scan
Units		2000	3000	1800
	(£)	(£)	(£)	(£)
Contribution	690 800	176 000	261 000	253 800
Fixed costs	(450 000)			
Maximum profit	240 800			

Therefore, since the maximum profit would be reduced the firm should not implement the proposal.

(a) **Question 10.16**

	Chairs	Benches	Tables	Total
Timber required per unit (m²)	2.5(£5/£2)	7.5(£15/£2)	5(£10/£2)	
Budgeted sales volume (units)	4 000	2 000	1 500	
Total timber required (m²)	10 000	15 000	7 500	32 500

Production requirements exceed the available supply of materials by 12 500 m².

	Chairs	Benches	Tables
Unit contributions (£)	8	17.50	16
Timber requirements (m²)	2.5	7.5	5
Contribution per m² (£)	3.2	2.33	3.20
Ranking	1	3	1

The scarce materials should be allocated as follows:

	Materials used	Balance unused
Chairs (4000 units × 2.5)	10 000	10 000
Tables (1500 units × 5)	7 500	2 500
Benches (2500/7.5 = 333 units)	2 500	—

The above production plan is sufficient to meet the order that has already been accepted. The profit arising from the above production plan is calculated as follows:

	(£)
Chairs (4000 units × £8 contribution)	32 000
Tables (1500 units × £16 contribution)	24 000
Benches (333 units × £17.50 contribution)	5 827
Total contribution	61 827
Fixed overheads (4000 × £4.50) + (2000 × £11.25) + (1500 × £9)	54 000
Profit	7 827

(b) The above production plan indicates that maximum sales demand for chairs and tables has been met but there is unutilized demand for benches. Therefore any additional materials purchased will be used to make benches yielding a contribution per unit sold of £17.50 and contribution per metre of material used of £2.33 (see part (a) for calculation). The company should not pay above £2.33 in excess of the acquisition cost of materials. The maximum purchase price is £4.33 (£2 + £2.33).

(c) See Chapter 2 for an explanation of each of the items listed in the question.

Question 10.17 (a)

The constraints on producing Part A are:

Line S = 6666 units (4000/0.6 hrs)
Line T = 9000 units (4500/0.5 hrs)
Material restriction = 8125 units (13 000/1.6 kg)
Therefore the constraint of Line S limits production to 6666 units

The constraints on producing Part B are:

Line S = 16 000 units (4000/0.25 hrs)
Line T = 8182 units (4500/0.55 hrs)
Material restriction = 8125 units (13 000/1.6 kg)
Maximum production of Part B is 8125 units

Maximum contributions for Parts A and B are:

	Part A (£)		Part B (£)	
Line S machine time	48	(0.6 hrs × £80)	20	(0.25 hrs × £80)
Line T machine time	50	(0.5 hrs × £100)	55	(0.55 hrs × £100)
Materials	20	(1.6 kg × £12.50)	20	(1.6 kg × £12.50)
Variable cost	118		95	
Selling price	145		115	
Unit contribution	27		20	
Maximum output	6666	units	8125	units
Maximum contribution	£79 982		£162 500	

Therefore Part A should be produced since it yields the largest contribution.

(b) The company will earn a contribution of £179 982 but it cannot meet the maximum call off due to the limitations of Line S.

(c)

	Part A		Part B	
Original selling price	145		115	
10% reduction in selling price	14.50		11.50	
Revised unit contribution	12.50	(£27 − £14.50)	8.50	(£20 − £11.50)
Output	6666	units	8125	units
Total contribution	£83 325		£69 062	
Payment for unused machine hours[a]	£70 020		£120 000	
Revised contribution	£153 345		£189 062	

Note
[a]The payment for unused machine hours is calculated as follows:

	Part A (£)	
Line S at £60 per hour	—	(Fully used)
Line T at £60 per hour	70 020	(4500 − [6666 × 0.5 hrs])
	70 020	

	Part B (£)	
Line S at £60 per hour	118 125	(4000 − [8125 × 0.25 hrs])
Line T at £60 per hour	1 875	(4500 − [8125 × 0.55 hrs])
	120 000	

With the alternative pricing arrangement the company should produce Part B.

Task 1

(a) and (b)

	£60	£70	£80	£90
Selling price	£60	£70	£80	£90
Sales volume (units)	25 000	20 000	16 000	11 000
	(£ per unit)	(£ per unit)	(£ per unit)	(£ per unit)
Direct material	14.00	14.00	14.00	16.10 (£14 × 115/100)
Direct labour	13.00	13.00	11.70 (90%)	11.70
Variable production overhead	4.00	4.00	4.00	4.00
Sales commission (10% of selling price)	6.00	7.00	8.00	9.00
Total variable cost per unit	37.00	38.00	37.70	40.80
Contribution per unit	23.00	32.00	42.30	49.20
	£000	£000	£000	£000
Total contribution	575	640	676.8	541.2
Fixed costs:				
production overhead (25 000 × £8)	200	200	190	190
selling and distribution (25 000 × £3)	75	70	70	70
administration (25 000 × £2)	50	50	50	50
Total fixed costs	325	320	310	310
Total annual profit	250	320	366.8	231.2

Task 2

(a) A selling price of £80 maximizes company profits at £366 800 per annum.

(b) Factors to be considered include:

(i) The effect on morale arising from a large reduction in direct labour and the resulting redundancies.

(ii) If competitors do not increase their prices customers may migrate to competitors in the long term and long-term annual profits may be considerably less than the profits predicted in the above schedule. The migration of customers may also enable competitors to reap the benefits of economies of scale thus resulting in their having lower unit costs than Rane Ltd.

Task 3

(a) The products should first be ranked according to their contribution per component used.

	Product A £ per unit	Product B £ per unit	Product C £ per unit	Product D £ per unit
Selling price	14	12	16	17
Variable costs	11	11	12	12
Contribution	3	1	4	5
Number of components used per unit	2 (£4/£2)	1 (£2/£2)	3 (£6/£2)	4 (£8/£2)
Contribution per component	£1.50	£1.00	£1.33	£1.25
Ranking	1	4	2	3

The scarce components should be allocated as follows:

Product	Units	Components used	Balance unused
A	4000	8 000	14 400
C	3600	10 800	3 600
D	900	3 600	—
		22 400	

(b) Profit to be earned next period:

Product	Units	Contribution per unit (£)	Total (£)
A	4000	3	12 000
C	3600	4	14 400
D	900		4 500
Total contribution			30 900
Fixed costs			8 000
Profit			22 900

Question 10.21 (a)

	Product X	Product Y	Total
(1) Estimated demand (000 units)	315	135	
(2) Machine hours required (per 000 units)	160	280	
(3) Machine hours required to meet demand (1 × 2)	50 400	37 800	88 200

The machine hours required to meet demand are in excess of the machine hours that are available. Therefore machine hours are the limiting factor and the company should allocate capacity according to contribution per machine hour.

	Product X (£)	Product Y (£)
Selling price	11.20	15.70
Variable cost	6.30	8.70
Contribution	4.90	7.00
Machine hours required per unit[a]	0.16	0.28
Contribution per machine hour	£30.625	£25

Note:
[a] Product X = 160/1000   Product Y = 280/1000

The company should concentrate on maximizing output of Product X. Meeting the maximum demand of Product X will require 50 400 machine hours and this will leave 34 600 hours (85 000 hrs − 50 400 hrs) to be allocated to Product Y. Therefore 123 571 units (34 600 hrs/0.28 hrs) of Y and 315 000 units of X should be produced.

(b)

	Product X (£)	Product Y (£)	Total (£)
Contribution per unit	4.90	7.00	
Sales volume	315 000	123.571	
Contribution (£000s)	1543.5	864.997	2 408.497
Less fixed costs[a]			2 124.997
Profit			283.500

Note:
[a] Fixed costs: Product X = 315 000 units × £4 per unit   = £1 260 000
Product Y = 123 571 units × £7 per unit   =   £864 997
2 124 997

(c) There are now two limiting factors and linear programming techniques must be used.

Let   X = Number of units of X produced (in 000s of units)
           Y = Number of units of Y produced (in 000s of units)

$160X + 280Y = 85\ 000$ Machine hours   (1)
$120X + 140Y = 55\ 000$ Labour hours   (2)

Multiply equation (2) by 2 and equation (1) by 1

$160X + 280Y = 85\ 000$ (1)
$240X + 280Y = 110\ 000$ (2)

Subtract equation (2) from equation (1)

$-80X = -25\ 000$
$X = 312.5$ (i.e. 312 500 units)

Substitute for X in equation (1)

$160\ (312.5) + 280Y = 85\ 000$
$50\ 000 + 280Y = 85\ 000$
$280Y = 35\ 000$
$Y = 125$ (i.e. 125 000 units)

Therefore the optimal output to fully utilize both labour and machine capacity is 312 500 units of Product X and 125 000 units of Product Y.

Activity-based costing

Solutions to Chapter 11 questions

Question summary

11.1–11.4 Essay and discussion questions.
11.5–11.9 The computation and comparison of
product costs derived from traditional

and activity-based costing approaches.
Question 11.7 requires comments on
results of the two systems.

Question 11.2 The answer to the question should describe the two-stage overhead allocation process and indicate that most cost systems use direct labour hours in the second stage. In today's production environment direct labour costs have fallen to about 10% of total costs for many firms and it is argued that direct labour is no longer a suitable base for assigning overheads to products. Using direct labour encourages managers to focus on reducing direct labour costs when they represent only a small percentage of total costs.

Approaches which are being adopted include:

(i) Changing from a direct labour overhead-recovery rate to recovery methods based on machine time. The justification for this is that overheads are caused by machine time rather than direct labour hours and cost.

(ii) Implementing activity-based costing systems that use many different cost drivers in the second stage of the two-stage overhead allocation procedure.

The answer should then go on to describe the benefits of ABC outlined in Chapter 11. Attention should also be drawn to the widespread use of direct labour hours by Japanese companies. According to Hiromoto[1] Japanese companies allocate overhead costs using the direct labour cost/hours to focus design engineers' attention on identifying opportunities to reduce the products' labour content. They use direct labour to encourage designers to make greater use of technology because this frequently improves long-term competitiveness by increasing quality, speed and flexibility of manufacturing.

Question 11.6 (a) (i) *Conventional Absorption Costing Profit Statement:*

		XYI	YZT	ABW
(1)	Sales volume (000 units)	50	40	30
		£	£	£
(2)	Selling price per unit	45	95	73
(3)	Prime cost per unit	32	84	65
(4)	Contribution per unit	13	11	8

---

[1] Hiromoto, T. (1988) 'Another hidden edge – Japanese management accounting'. *Harvard Business Review*, July/August, pp. 22–6.

(5) Total contribution in £000s (1 × 4)	650	440	240
(6) Machine department overheads[a]	120	240	144
(7) Assembly department overheads[b]	288.75	99	49.5
Profit (£000s)	241.25	101	46.5

Total profit = £388 750

Notes:
[a] XYI = 50 000 × 2 hrs × £1.20, YZT = 40 000 × 5 hrs × £1.20
[b] XYI = 50 000 × 7 hrs × £0.825, YZT = 40 000 × 3 hrs × £0.825

(ii) *Cost pools:*

	Machining services	Assembly services	Set-ups	Order processing	Purchasing
£000	357	318	26	156	84
Cost drivers	420 000 machine hours	530 000 direct labour hours	520 set-ups	32 000 customer orders	11 200 suppliers' orders
Cost driver rates	£0.85 per machine hour	£0.60 per direct labour hour	£50 per set-up	£4.875 per customer order	£7.50 per suppliers' order

ABC Profit Statement:

	XYI (£000)	YZT (£000)	ABW (£000)
Total contribution	650	440	240
Less overheads:			
Machine department at £0.85 per hour	85	170	102
Assembly at £0.60 per hour	210	72	36
Set-up costs at £50 per set-up	6	10	10
Order processing at £4.875 per order	39	39	78
Purchasing at £7.50 per order	22.5	30	31.5
Profit (Loss)	287.5	119	(17.5)

Total profit = £389 000

(b) See the section on a comparison of ABC and traditional product costs in Chapter 11 for the answer to this question.

Question 11.7

(a) Direct labour cost for the period = (7500 units × £4) + (12 500 units × £8) + (4000 units × £6.40) = £155 600

Direct labour cost percentage overhead rate = $\dfrac{\text{Total overheads (£718 688)}}{\text{Direct labour cost (£155 600)}}$ × 100 = 462%

Unit product costs (Existing costing system)

	P1 (£)	P2 (£)	P3 (£)
Direct labour	4.00	8.00	6.40
Direct materials	18.00	25.00	16.00
Overheads (462% of direct labour cost)	18.48	36.96	29.57
Unit cost	40.48	69.96	51.97
Selling price	47.00	80.00	68.00
Profit margin	6.52	10.04	16.03

(b)

Unit product costs (ABC system)

	P1 (£)	P2 (£)	P3 (£)
Direct labour	4.00	8.00	6.40
Direct materials	18.00	25.00	16.00
Total direct costs	22.00	33.00	22.40
Overhead costs:			
Receiving/materials handling (1)	1.01	3.80	23.73
Maintenance and depreciation (2)	18.06	18.06	7.22
Set-up labour (3)	0.16	0.47	2.92
Engineering (4)	4.00	1.60	12.50
Packing (5)	0.27	1.12	11.00
Total overhead costs	23.50	25.05	57.37
Total unit cost	45.50	58.05	79.77
Selling price	47.00	80.00	68.00
Profit margin	1.50	21.95	(11.77)

Workings:
(1) Receiving and handling of materials:
    Cost driver = Number of material movements = 79 (4 + 25 + 50)
    Cost per material movement = £1898.73 (£150 000/79)
    Cost per unit for P1 = (£1898.73 × 4)/7500 = £1.01
(2) Maintenance and depreciation cost:
    Cost driver = Number of machine hours = 10 800 [(0.5 × 7500) + (0.5 × 12 500) + (0.2 × 4 000)]
    Cost per machine hour = £36.11 (£390 000/10 800)
    Cost per unit for P1 = £18.06 (£36.11 × 0.5)
(3) Set-up labour cost:
    Cost driver = Number of set-ups = 16 (1 + 5 + 10)
    Cost per set-up = £1168 (£18 688/16)
    Cost per unit for P1 = £0.16 (£1168 × 1)/7500
(4) Engineering cost:
    Cost driver = Proportion of engineering work
    Cost per unit for P1 = £4 (£100 000 × 30%)/7500
(5) Packing cost:
    Cost driver = Number of orders packed = 30 (1 +7 + 22)
    Cost per order = £2000 (£60 000/30)
    Cost per unit for P1 = £0.27 (£2000 × 1)/7500

The above calculations are for P1 only. The unit costs for P2 and P3 would be calculated in a similar manner. An alternative approach to answering the question is to allocate the total costs based on the proportions of the cost drivers consumed by each product and derive the unit costs by dividing total costs by the output for each product as follows:

	Total (£)	P1 (£)	P2 (£)	P3 (£)
Receiving and handling	150 000	7 595	47 468	94 937
Maintenance/depreciation	390 000	135 417	225 694	28 889
Set-up labour	18 688	1 168	5 840	11 680
Engineering	100 000	30 000	20 000	50 000
Packing	60 000	2 000	14 000	44 000
Sub total overhead costs	718 688	176 180	313 002	229 506
Number of units		7 500	12 500	4 000
Unit overhead cost (£)		£23.49	£25.04	£57.38

(c) P1 has higher unit costs and a lower profit margin with the ABC system. This is caused by its relatively higher proportion of machine usage compared with other products. Also because it is the least labour intensive product the existing system, that allocates all the overheads on the basis of direct labour costs, is likely to undercost it. The low profit margin raises questions about changing the product mix and concentrating on more profitable products if the price P2 cannot be increased or its costs reduced.

P3 appears to be a complex product to make. It is made in small batches and, relative to other products, the order sizes are small. This cost of this complexity is not captured by the existing traditional costing system that relies on a single volume-based cost driver. In contrast, by using different types of volume and non-volume-based cost drivers the ABC system captures the cost of the complexity of P3. Therefore considerably more overheads are assigned to P3 by the ABC system compared with the existing traditional system. Indeed, the traditional system reports the highest profit margin whereas the ABC system reports a loss for P3. It is not surprising that this product is attracting additional business because it is being priced below its total cost. There is a need to either increase the selling price or reduce the resources consumed, and thus the costs, of P3. The ABC system draws attention to why costs are being incurred. By reducing the number of material movements, delivering in larger batch sizes and reducing engineering work it may be possible to reduce the costs of P3 so that it becomes profitable. If it is not possible to either increase price and/or reduce costs serious consideration should be given to discontinuing P3.

P2 is a labour intensive product and since the existing system allocates overheads on the basis of labour costs it is being over-costed by the existing system. Although it is a high volume product it consumes relatively less support resources (particularly receiving/materials handling, engineering and packing) than P3. It is likely that the loss of market share is due to P2 being over-costed and thus over-priced. This is reflected in a loss of market share as competitors have discovered that they can manufacture and sell the product at a lower price than BML and still make a profit.

(a) For the answer to this question see Chapter 11.

Question 11.8

(b) *Machine-related costs*
Machine hours for the period:

$$
\begin{array}{llr}
A = 500 \times \frac{1}{4} & = & 125 \\
B = 5000 \times \frac{1}{4} & = & 1\,250 \\
C = 600 \times 1 & = & 600 \\
D = 7000 \times 1\frac{1}{2} & = & 10\,500 \\
\hline
& & 12\,475
\end{array}
$$

Machine hour rate = £3 per hour (£37 424/12 475 hrs)

Set-up related costs
Cost per set-up = £256.18 (£4355/17)
Set-up cost per unit of output:

$$
\begin{array}{lll}
\text{Product A } (1 \times £256.18)/500 & = £0.51 \\
B (6 \times £256.18)/5000 & = £0.31 \\
C (2 \times £256.18)/600 & = £0.85 \\
D (8 \times £256.18)/7000 & = £0.29
\end{array}
$$

Material ordering related costs
Cost per order = £1920/10 orders = £192 per order
Material ordering cost per unit of output:

$$
\begin{array}{lll}
\text{Product A } (1 \times £192)/500 & = £0.38 \\
\text{B } (4 \times £192)/5000 & = £0.15 \\
\text{C } (1 \times £192)/600 & = £0.32 \\
\text{D } (4 \times £192)/7000 & = £0.11
\end{array}
$$

Material handling related costs
Cost per material handing = £7580/27 = £280.74
Material handling cost per unit of output:

$$
\begin{array}{lll}
\text{Product A } (2 \times £280.74)/500 & = £1.12 \\
\text{B } (10 \times £280.74)/5000 & = £0.56 \\
\text{C } (3 \times £280.74)/600 & = £1.40 \\
\text{D } (12 \times £280.74)/7000 & = £0.48
\end{array}
$$

Spare parts
Cost per part = £8600/12 = £716.67
Administration of spare parts cost per unit of output:

$$
\begin{array}{lll}
\text{Product A } (2 \times £716.67)/500 & = £2.87 \\
\text{B } (5 \times £716.67)/5000 & = £0.72 \\
\text{C } (1 \times £716.67)/600 & = £1.19 \\
\text{D } (4 \times £716.67)/7000 & = £0.41
\end{array}
$$

Overhead cost per unit of output

Product	A (£)	B (£)	C (£)	D (£)
ABC overhead cost:				
Machine overheads	0.75	0.75	3.00	4.50
Set-ups	0.51	0.31	0.85	0.29
Material ordering	0.38	0.15	0.32	0.11
Material handling	1.12	0.56	1.40	0.48
Spare parts	2.87	0.72	1.19	0.41
	5.63	2.49	6.76	5.79
Present system	1.20	1.20	4.80	7.20
Difference	+4.43	+1.29	+1.96	−1.41

The present system is based on the assumption that all overhead expenditure is volume-related, measured in terms of machine hours. However, the overheads for the five support activities listed in the question are unlikely to be related to machine hours. Instead, they are related to the factors that influence the spending on support activities (i.e. the cost drivers). The ABC system traces costs to products based on the quantity (cost drivers) of activities consumed. Product D is the high volume product, and thus the present volume-based system traces a large share of overheads to this product. In contrast, the ABC system recognizes that product D consumes overheads according to activity consumption and traces a lower amount of overhead to this product. The overall effect is that, with the present system, product D is overcosted and the remaining products are undercosted. For a more detailed explanation of the difference in resource consumption between products for an ABC and traditional cost system see 'A comparison of traditional and ABC systems' and 'Volume-based and non-volume-based cost drivers' in Chapter 11 for the answer to this question.

Capital investment decisions

Solutions to Chapter 12 questions

Question summary

Question 12.1

(a) (i) Annual cash flow = Annual profit + Annual depreciation (£15 000).
The annual cash flows for each project are as follows:

Year	Project 1	Project 2
1	45 000	40 000
2	45 000	30 000
3	35 000	35 000
4	5 000	35 000
5	5 000	0

$$\text{Payback period} = 1 + \frac{75 - 45}{45} \qquad 2 + \frac{75 - 70}{35}$$

$$= 1.7 \text{ years} = 2.1 \text{ years}$$

(ii)

	Cash flow (£)	Discount factor	Project 1 PV (£)	Cash flow (£)	Project 2 PV (£)
Outlay	(75 000)	1	(75 000)	(75 000)	(75 000)
Year 1	45 000	0.869	39 105	40 000	34 760
2	45 000	0.756	34 020	30 000	22 680
3	35 000	0.657	22 995	35 000	22 995
4	5 000	0.571	2 855	35 000	19 985
5	5 000	0.497	2 485	–	–
PV Inflows			£101 460		£100 420
NPV			£26 460		£25 420

(b) See sections on the concept of NPV and payback methods in Chapter 12 for the answer to this question.

(c) Both the NPV and payback methods indicate that the firm should choose Project 1.

Question 12.3 (a) This part of the question requires you to focus on the new machine only and does not require a decision as to which machine should be purchased. Depreciation should not be included in the analysis because it is already included in the investment cost. Allocated costs are not relevant costs. The net cash inflow per unit is £1.75 (£3 – £1.25).

	Net cash inflow (£)	Discount factor	Present value (£)
Year 1	70 000 (40,000 × £1.75)	0.833	58 310
2	70 000	0.694	48 580
3	52 500	0.579	30 398
4	35 000	0.482	16 870
5	35 000	0.402	14 070
			168 228
		Investment cost	(150 000)
		NPV	18 228

(i) Payback period: Cumulative cash inflows are £140 000 by the end of year 2 and a further £10 000 is required to repay the initial cost. Therefore the payback period is 2 years plus £10 000/£52 500 or 2.19 years.
(ii) NPV = £18.228.

(b) The cash inflows are represented by the savings in relevant operating costs of £0.25 per unit (£1.50 – £1.25) and the sale proceeds from the old machine of £130 000.

	Net cash inflow (£)	Discount factor	Present value (£)
Year 0	130 000	1.000	130 000
1	10 000 (40 000 × £0.25)	0.833	8 330
2	10 000	0.694	6 940
3	7 500	0.579	4 342
4	5 000	0.482	2 410
5	5 000	0.402	2 010
			154 032
		Investment cost	(150 000)
		NPV	4 032

(c) Factors to be considered:
(i) The quality of fruit pies.
(ii) The reliability and speed of delivery service.
(iii) The possibility of future price increases.
(iv) The number of suppliers. If there are few suppliers the group might be entirely dependent on the supplier who may take advantage of the situation.
(v) The impact on the work force. Will there be any redundancies? Is there high unemployment in the area?

(a) The answer should stress that NPV is considered superior to the payback method **Question 12.5** and the accounting rate of return because it takes account of the time value of money. For a description of the time value of money you should refer to 'Compounding and discounting' and 'The concept of net present value' in Chapter 12. The answer should also draw attention to the limitations of the payback method and accounting rate of return described in Chapter 12.

(b) (i) To compute the NPV it is necessary to convert the profits into cash flows by adding back depreciation of £25 000 per annum in respect of the asset purchased at the end of year 3 for £75 000. The NPV calculation is as follows:

Year	Cash flow (£)	Discount factor	NPV
3	(75 000)	0.675	(50 625)
4	35 000	0.592	20 720
5	28 000	0.519	14 532
6	27 000	0.465	12 555
			(2 818)

(ii) The cash flows are based on the assumption that the reinvestment in R is not made at the end of year 3.

Year	Discount factor	Project T cash flows[a] (£)	Project T NPV (£)	Project R cash flows (£)	Project R NPV (£)
1	0.877	27 000	23 679	40 000 (3)[c]	35 080
2	0.769	30 000	23 070	45 000	34 605
3	0.675	32 000	21 600	45 000 (4)[d]	30 375
4	0.592	44 000	26 048		
5	0.519	40 000[b]	20 760		
			115 157		100 060
Investment outlay			70 000		60 000
NPV			45 157		40 060

Payback: $T = 2$ years $+ (£70\,000 - £57\,000)/£32\,000 = 2.41$ years
$R = 1$ year $+ (£60\,000 - £40\,000)/45\,000 = 1.44$ years

The decision should be to invest in Project T because it has the higher NPV.

Notes
[a] Yearly profits plus (£70 000 − £10 000)/5 years depreciation.
[b] £18 000 profits + £12 000 depreciation + £10 000 sale proceeds.
[c] Profits plus £60 000/3 years depreciation.
[d] £75 000 investment outlay − £50 000 = Annual profit (£25 000). Cash flow = £25 000 profit + £20 000 depreciation.

(c) For an explanation of the meaning of the term 'discount rate' see 'The opportunity cost of an investment' in Chapter 12. The discount rate can be derived from observations of the returns shareholders require in financial markets. Where a project is to be financed fully by borrowing, the cost of borrowing could be used as a basis for determining the discount rate.

Question 12.6 (i) Net present values:

Year	0% NPV (£)	10% Discount Factor	10% NPV (£)	20% Discount Factor	20% NPV (£)
0	(142 700)	1 000	(142 700)	1.000	(142 700)
1	51 000	0.909	46 359	0.833	42 483
2	62 000	0.826	51 212	0.694	43 028
3	73 000	0.751	54 823	0.579	42 267
NPV	43 300		9 694		(14 922)

(ii)

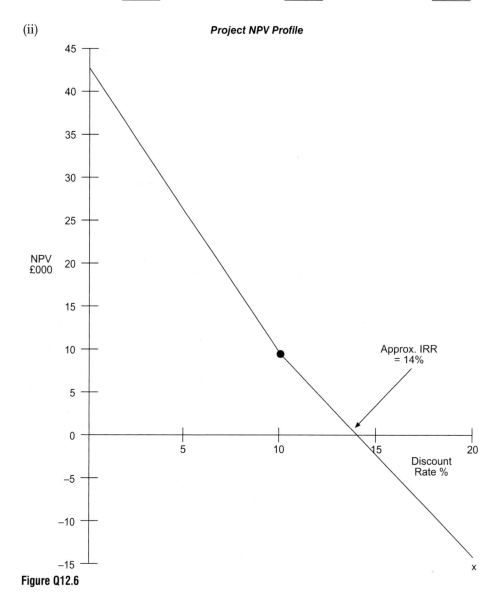

Project NPV Profile

Approx. IRR = 14%

Figure Q12.6

(a) Payback and net present value are techniques which focus on cash flows rather than profits. The investment outlay is brought into the analysis as a cash flow. Depreciation should not therefore be included in the analysis as this would involve double counting. The accounting rate of return measures average profit as a percentage return on the average investment over a project's life. Because the focus is on profits, and not cash flows, depreciation should be included in the accounting rate of return computation.

(b) (i) *Payback:*
Project 1 = 2 years (£150 000 – £110 000)/£45 000 = 2.89 years
Project 2 = 3 years (£150 000 – £137 000)/£49 000 = 3.27 years

(ii) *Accounting rate of return:*

	Project 1	Project 2
Average profits	£32 500 (£130 000/4)	£28 000 (£140 000/5)
Average investment (1)	£110 000	£90 000
Accounting rate of return	30%	31%

Note:
(1) Average investment = (½ Investment outlay) + (½ Disposal value)

(iii) *Net present value:*

Year	Discount Factor	Project 1 Cash flow (£)	Project 1 Present value (£)	Project 2 Cash flow (£)	Project 2 Present value (£)
1	0.869	60 000	52 140	54 000	46 926
2	0.756	50 000	37 800	44 000	33 264
3	0.659	45 000	29 655	39 000	25 701
4	0.571	125 000	71 375	49 000	27 979
5	0.497			104 000	51 688
			190 970		185 558
Less investment outlay			150 000		150 000
NPV			40 970		35 558

The decision should be based on the NPV method and Project 1 should be chosen.

(c) The NPV method computes the present value of cash flows. Depreciation is not a cash flow whereas the disposal value at the end of the project's life is a cash flow. The payback method also focuses on cash flows and the disposal value is required to determine the average investment to compute the accounting rate of return.

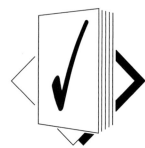

The budgeting process

Solutions to Chapter 13 questions

Question 13.1

		(£)
September sales	(£100 000 × 0.5 × 0.97)	48 500
August sales	(£60 000 × 0.30)	18 000
July sales	(£80 000 × 0.15)	12 000
		78 500

Answer = D

Question 13.6

(a)

Product	A		B		C	Total
Sales mix weighting	1		2		4	
	(£)		(£)		(£)	(£)
Unit selling price	215		250		300	
Unit costs:						
Frame	20		20		20	
Component D (at £8 per unit)	40		8		24	
E (at £5 per unit)	5		35		25	
F (at £3 per unit)	12	57	15	58	3	52
Labour:						
Skilled (at £6 per hour)	12		9		9	
Unskilled (at £4.50 per hour)	9	21	9	18	13.5	22.5
Variable production overhead		5		4		3.5
Contribution		112		150		202
Weighted by sales mix		112		300		808	1220

Required period 1 contribution:	(£m)
Profit	0.500 (£6.5m/13)
Add fixed costs:	
Production	0.056 (£0.728m/13)
Selling and distribution	0.028 (£0.364m/13)
Administration	0.026 (£0.338m/13)
	0.610

∴ 500 (£610 000/£1220) 'mixes' must be sold each period.

(i) *Sales budget*

	A	B	C
Sales quantities	500	1 000	2 000
Sales value (£)	107 500	250 000	600 000

(ii) *Production budget*

	A	B	C
Sales quantities	500	1000	2000
Closing stock	270	630	1440
	770	1630	3440
Opening stock	300	700	1600
Production	470	930	1840

(iii) *Material usage budget*

				Total (units)
Usage:				
Frame	470	930	1 840	3 240
D	2 350	930	5 520	8 800
E	470	6 510	9 200	16 180
F	1 880	4 650	1 840	8 370

(iv) *Purchases budget*

Purchases (units):	Frame	D	E	F
Closing stock	900	3 600	9 000	3 600
Add used in production	3 240	8 800	16 180	8 370
	4 140	12 400	25 180	11 970
Less opening stock	1 000	4 000	10 000	4 000
Purchases (units)	3 140	8 400	15 180	7 970
Cost (£)	62 800	67 200	75 900	23 910

(v) *Manpower budgets*

	Machining (hours)	Assembly (hours)
A (units produced × hrs per unit)	940	940
B	1395	1860
C	2760	5520
	5095	8320
Hours available per period (4 × 37.5)	150	150
Number of people required	34	56

(b) The following factors would need to be considered:

  (i) The ability to be able to plan future production requirements, since production might be halted if there was a sudden increase in production. If production is volatile, there is a danger that stockouts might occur.

  (ii) The speed and reliability of the delivery service. If suppliers can deliver at short notice then stockouts are less likely to occur.

  (iii) The extra costs involved arising from more frequent deliveries in terms of ordering costs and quantity discounts.

  (iv) Alternative use of storage space.

  (v) The savings in holding costs arising from the reduction in stocks. Stock reductions in units would be as follows:

	Frames	D	E	F
End of period 1	900	3600	9000	3600
Requirements for 1 week	810 (3240/4)	2200 (8800/4)	4045 (16 180/4)	2092 (8370/4)
Stock reduction	90	1400	4955	1508

Question 13.7 *Task 1*

(a) *Production budget – third quarter ending 17 September*

	Alphas	Betas
Budgeted sales in units	2000	2400
Add closing stock[a]	200	480
Less opening stock (given)	(500)	(600)
Production of completed units	1700	2280

(b) *Materials purchases budget – third quarter ending 17 September*

	kilograms
Material required for Alpha production (8kg × 1700)	13 600
Material required for Beta production (12kg × 2280)	27 360
	40 960
Add closing material stock[b]	16 384
Less opening material stock (given)	(12 000)
Material purchases	45 344

(c) *Cost of material purchases* (45 344 × £10)   £453 440

(d) *Labour budget – third quarter ending 17 September*

Labour hours required for Alpha production (3 hours × 1700)	5 100
Labour hours required for Beta production (6 hours × 2280)	13 680
Total hours required before efficiency adjustment	18 780
Efficiency adjustment ($^{20\%}/_{80\%}$)	4 695
Total labour hours	23 475
Normal hours (50 employees × 35 hours × 12 weeks)	21 000
Overtime hours	2 475

(e)

Normal hours (50 employees × 12 weeks × £210)	£126 000
Overtime (2475 hours × £9)	£22 275
Cost of labour	£148 275

Notes	*Alphas*	*Betas*
[a]Sales this quarter	2000	2400
Add 20% seasonal variation	400	480
Budgeted sales next quarter	2400	2880
Closing stock (5/60 × 2400 = 200) (10/60 × 2880 = 480)	200	480

[b]Closing stock of materials	
Production this period	40 960
Add 20%	8 192
Material required for production next period	49 152
Stock required (20/60 × 49 152)	16 384

Task 2

(a) Some of the following limitations should be included in the report:
   (i) Past data are normally used as a basis for determining the linear regression formula. If only a small number of past observations are available the resulting regression formula is not likely to be very accurate.
   (ii) The technique assumes that a linear relationship exists whereas in practice a curvilinear relationship may exist.

(iii) If past data are used to make future predictions it is assumed that the past trend will continue into the future. However, past trends may suddenly change for a variety of reasons.

(iv) If abnormal observations are included in past data the regression equation will not be typical of future normal relationships.

Task 2

(b) The report should identify the following alternative methods of forecasting:
   (i) Market research involving customer surveys of likely future demand.
   (ii) Obtaining estimates from salespersons who deal with the customers and who have the knowledge to predict future demand.

Task 1

Question 13.8

Alderley Ltd Budget Statements 13 weeks to 4 April

(a) Production Budget

	Elgar units	Holst units
Budgeted sales volume	845	1235
Add closing stock[a]	78	1266
Less Opening stock	(163)	(361)
Units of production	760	1140

(b) Material Purchases Budget

	Elgar kg	Holst kg	Total kg
Material consumed	5320 (760 × 7)	9120 (1140 × 8)	14 440
Add raw material closing stock[b]			2 888
Less raw material opening stock			(2 328)
Purchases (kg)			15 000

(c) Purchases (£) (1500 × £12)   £180 000

(d) Production Labour Budget

	Elgar hours	Holst hours	Total hours
Standard hours produced[c]	6080	5700	11 780
Productivity adjustment (5/95 × 11 780)			620
Total hours employed			12 400
Normal hours employed[d]			11 544
Overtime hours			856

(e) Labour cost

	£
Normal hours (11 544 × £8)	92 352
Overtime (856 × £8 × 125%)	8 560
Total	100 912

Notes:
[a] Number of days per period = 13 weeks × 5 days = 65
   Stock: Elgar = (6/65) × 845 = 78, Holst = (14/65) × 1235 = 266
[b] (13/65) × (5320 + 9120) = 2888
[c] Elgar 760 × 8 hours = 6080, Holst 1140 × 5 hours = 5700
[d] 24 employees × 37 hours × 13 weeks = 11 544

Task 2

(a) Four ways of forecasting future sales volume are:
   (i) Where the number of customers is small it is possible to interview them to ascertain what their likely demand will be over the forecasting period.

(ii) Produce estimates based on the opinion of executives and sales personnel. For example, sales personnel may be asked to estimate the sales of each product to their customers, or regional sales managers may estimate the total sales for each of their regions.

(iii) Market research may be necessary where it is intended to develop new products or new markets. This may involve interviews with existing and potential customers in order to estimate potential demand.

(iv) Estimates involving statistical techniques that incorporate general business and market conditions and past growth in sales.

(b) Interviewing customers and basing estimates on the opinions of sales personnel are likely to be more appropriate for existing products and customers involving repeat sales. Market research is appropriate for new products or markets and where the market is large and anticipated revenues are likely to be sufficient to justify the cost of undertaking the research.

Statistical estimates derived from past data are likely to be appropriate where conditions are likely to be stable and past demand patterns are likely to be repeated through time. This method is most suited to existing products or markets where sufficient data is available to establish a trend in demand.

(c) The major limitation of interviewing customers is that they may not be prepared to divulge the information if their future plans are commercially sensitive. There is also no guarantee that the orders will be placed with Alderley Ltd. They may place their orders with competitors.

Where estimates are derived from sales personnel there is a danger that they might produce over-optimistic estimates in order to obtain a favourable performance rating at the budget setting stage. Alternatively, if their future performance is judged by their ability to achieve the budgeted sales they may be motivated to underestimate sales demand.

Market research is expensive and may produce unreliable estimates if inexperienced researchers are used. Also small samples are often used which may not be indicative of the population and this can result in inaccurate estimates.

Statistical estimates will produce poor demand estimates where insufficient past data is available, demand is unstable over time and the future environment is likely to be significantly different from the past. Statistical estimates are likely to be inappropriate for new products and new markets where past data is unavailable.

Question 13.10 (a) *Monthly cash budget*

	Month 1 (£000)	Month 2 (£000)	Month 3 (£000)	Month 4 (£000)
Cash inflows:				
Sales (W1)	24.0	93.6	92.6	90.7
Cash outflows:				
Business purchase	315.0	—	—	—
Delivery van	—	15.0	—	—
Raw materials (W2)	—	44.375	29.375	30.625
Direct labour (W2)	27.0	17.25	18.0	18.75
Production overhead (W3)	10.5	10.5	10.5	10.5
Selling and administration overhead (W4)	39.875	14.875	14.875	14.875
	392.375	102.0	72.75	74.75
Surplus/(deficit) for month	(368.375)	(8.4)	19.85	15.95
Opening balance	—	(368.375)	(376.775)	(356.925)
Closing balance	(368.375)	(376.775)	(356.925)	(340.975)

Workings

	Month 1	Month 2	Month 3	Month 4
(W1) Cash inflow from sales	24	24	23	24
Cash inflow from credit sales	—	72	72	69
Less discount	—	(2.4)	(2.4)	(2.3)
	—	69.6	69.6	66.7
Total cash inflow	24	93.6	92.6	90.7

(W2) Selling price at a mark-up of 60% on production cost is £8 per unit (£5.00 × 1.60).

Sales units = sales revenue/8.

(000 units)	Month 1	Month 2	Month 3	Month 4	Month 5	Month 6
Sales	12	12	11.5	12	12.5	13
+ Closing stock of finished goods	12	11.5	12	12.5	13	
− Opening stock of finished goods	6	12	11.5	12	12.5	
= Production	18	11.5	12	12.5	13	
+ Closing stock of raw materials	5.75	6	6.25	6.5		
− Opening stock of raw materials	6	5.75	6	6.25		
= Purchase of raw materials	17.75	11.75	12.25	12.75		

Raw material cost (£000)	Month 1	Month 2	Month 3	Month 4
= Purchases at £2.50	44.375	29.375	30.265	31.875
Raw material payment (£000)	—	44.375	29.375	30.625
Direct labour cost and payment (£000)				
= Production × £1.50	27	17.25	18	18.75

(W3) Production overhead = £1.00 × 150 000 units
$$= £150\,000$$

Less depreciation	£24 000	(£120 000/5)
Annual payment	£126 000	
Monthly payment	£10 500	

(W4) Selling and administration overhead = £208 000

Less depreciation (year 1)	4 500	(£15 000 × 30%)
	203 500	
Less rent and rates	25 000	
Year 1 payment	178 500	(excluding rent and rates)
Monthly payment	£14 875	(plus £25 000 in month 1)

(b)

	(£)
Finished goods stock (12 500 units × £5 per unit)	62 500
Raw materials stock (6500 units × £2.50 per unit)	16 250
Debtors	69 600
	148 350
Creditors	31 875

Apart from the purchase of the business, the cash budget suggests that there will be sufficient cash inflows to meet the cash outflows. The current assets and debtors provide sufficient funds to cover the creditors. However, this does not take into account possible funding by bank overdraft to finance the business purchase.

Question 13.11 (a) (i) *Cash budget*

	January (£)	February (£)	March (£)	April (£)
Balance b/d	10 000	9 000	3 890	9 090
Sales (W1)	—	15 200	57 100	80 000
	10 000	24 200	60 990	89 090
Purchases (W3)	—	11 550	24 500	26 950
Wages (W4)	—	4 800	19 800	22 200
Variable overhead (W5)	—	960	4 600	7 080
Fixed overhead (W6)	1 000	3 000	3 000	3 000
	1 000	20 310	51 900	59 230
Balance c/d	9 000	3 890	9 090	29 860

Workings

(W1) Sales

	Amount	20%	Discount 5%	Net	50%	20%	8%	Total cash receipts
January	—	—	—	—	—	—	—	
February	80 000	16 000	800	15 200				15 200
March	90 000	18 000	900	17 100	40 000			57 100
April	100 000	20 000	1000	19 000	45 000	16 000		80 000
May	100 000	20 000	1000	19 000	50 000	18 000	6400	93 400

(W2) Production:

					Total
January	800				800
February	2400	900			3300
March		2700	1000		3700
April			3000	1000	4000
May				3000	
	3200	3600	4000	4000	

(W3) Purchases at £7 per unit:

	Production	Current month	Following month	Total	Value (£)
January	February (3300)		1650	1650	11 550
February	March (3700)	1650	1850	3500	24 500
March	April (4000)	1850	2000	3850	26 950

(W4) Direct wages:

February payment	800 × £6 =	£4 800
March payment	3300 × £6 =	£19 800
April payment	3700 × £6 =	£22 200

(W5) Variable overhead at £2 per unit:

Production	February (£)	March (£)	April (£)	May (£)
January (£1600)	960	640		
February (£6600)		3960	2640	
March (£7400)			4440	2960
	960	4600	7080	2960

(W6) Fixed overhead:

	January (£)	February (£)	March (£)	April (£)
January	1000	2000		
February		1000	2000	
March			1000	2000
April				1000
	1000	3000	3000	3000

(ii) It is assumed that the question relates to the amount received from customers in May and not the amount due. The answer is £93 400 (see *W1*).

(b) A software package would eliminate the tedious arithmetical calculations that are necessary to produce cash budgets. Furthermore, it would enable alternative scenarios to be considered, such as what the outcome would be if any of the parameters were changed.

(a) Cash budget for the period April–June **Question 13.13**

	April (£000)	May (£000)	June (£000)	July (£000)
Receipts:				
Sales (1)	44 140	51 870	58 130	56 885
Payments:				
Materials (2)	15 478	17 010	16 673	15 635
Labour (3)	13 800	14 850	14 325	13 425
Variable overhead	7 200	7 500	7 050	6 600
Fixed overhead (4)	8 000	8 000	8 000	8 000
Administration overhead	500	500	500	500
Selling overhead	1 100	1 300	1 200	1 150
Machinery		15 000		
Corporation tax			10 000	
Dividends				7 500
Total payments	46 078	64 160	57 748	52 810
Balance brought forward	14 500	12 562	272	654
Receipts	44 140	51 870	58 130	56 885
	58 640	64 432	58 402	57 539
Payments	46 078	64 160	57 748	52 810
Closing balance carried forward	12 562	272	654	4 729

Workings:
(1) Sales receipts:

	April	May	June	July
Received in current month (Sales × .20 × .99)	10 890	12 870	11 880	11 385
55% in month after sale	24 750	30 250	35 750	33 000
15% in 2 months after sale	6 000	6 750	8 250	9 750
5% in 3 months after sale	2 500	2 000	2 250	2 750
	44 140	51 870	58 130	56 885

(2) Materials:

Purchases (unit cost × monthly production)	16 800	17 500	16 450	15 400
Payment in the current month (60% × .98 × purchase cost)	9 878	10 290	9 673	9 055
Payment 1 month in arrears (40% of purchase cost)	5 600	6 720	7 000	6 580
	15 478	17 010	16 673	15 635

(3) Labour:

Monthly cost (unit cost × monthly production)	14 400	15 000	14 100	13 200
Payment in the current month (75%)	10 800	11 250	10 575	9 900
Payment 1 month in arrears	3 000	3 600	3 750	3 525
	13 800	14 850	14 325	13 425

(4) Fixed overhead:
Monthly cost = (£8 × 14m units)/12 = £9.333m per month
Less depreciation of £16m/12
(non-cash expense) = £1.333 per month
Monthly cost = £8m per month

(b) See 'Feedback and Feedforward controls' in Chapter 14 for an explanation of these terms. Preparing the cash budget at the planning stage and taking appropriate remedial action at this stage to achieve the planned cash requirements represents feedforward control. Comparing actual cash balances with the cash budget and taking appropriate action where balances deviate from plan represents feedback control.

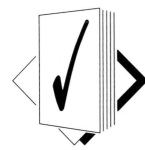

Management control systems

Solutions to Chapter 14 questions

Question 14.1

(a) See Chapter 14 for the answer to this question. In particular, your answer should stress:
 (i) The need for a system of responsibility accounting based on a clear definition of a manager's authority and responsibility.
 (ii) The production of performance reports at frequent intervals comparing actual and budget costs for individual expense items. Variances should be analysed according to whether they are controllable or non-controllable by the manager.
 (iii) The managers should participate in the setting of budgets and standards.
 (iv) The system should ensure that variances are investigated, causes found and remedial action is taken.
 (v) An effective cost control system must not be used as a punitive device, but should be seen as a system that helps managers to control their costs more effectively.

(b) Possible problems include:
 (i) Difficulties in setting standards for non-repetitive work.
 (ii) Non-acceptance by budgetees if they view the system as a punitive device to judge their performance.
 (iii) Isolating variances where interdependencies exist.

Question 14.7

Flexible budget at 85% activity

	(£)	(£)
Variable cost		
Direct materials[a]	1 386 056	
Direct wages[b]	2 356 949	
Variable production overhead[c]	489 584	
Variable selling and distribution overhead[d]	69 940	
		4 302 529
Fixed costs		
Fixed production overhead[c]	330 115	
Fixed selling and distribution overhead[d]	161 266	
Administration overhead	132 000	623 381
Total cost		4 925 910
Sales[e]		5 911 092
Profit		985 182

Notes

[a] Costs increase by £153 800 for each of the changes in activity. Thus at 85% capacity level costs will be (£1 153 800 + £153 800) 1.04 after taking account of the predicted price change of 4%.

[b] Costs have increased by increments of £269 150. At 85% capacity level predicted costs are (£2 019 150 + £269 150) 1.03.

[c] Costs have increased by increments of £53 830. However, the question indicates that there is a fixed and variable element. Therefore at 85% capacity variable costs are predicted to be 8.5 (10% increments) × £53 830 per 10% increment = £457 555 × 1.07 price increase = £489 584. The fixed cost element before the price increase is £703 830 total costs at 75% capacity less variable costs of 7.5 (10% increments) × £53 830 = £300 105. The predicted fixed costs after the price increase are £300 105 (1.10) = £330 115.

[d] Costs have increased in increments of £7690. Using the same principles as those outlined in [c] variable costs at 85% capacity are predicted to be 8.5 × £7690 (1.07 inflation factor) = £69 940. Fixed cost element = £207 690 total cost at 75% capacity less 7.5 (£7690) = £150 015 before the price increase. After the price increase the estimated fixed costs will be £150 015 (1.075) = £161 266.

[e] Total cost (£4 925 910) × 100/83.333.

(b) Problems that can arise from a change in capacity level include:
  1. Step increase in fixed costs to enable output to be expanded.
  2. Inability to sell the increased output resulting in an increase in stocks.
  3. Working the plant more intensively might result in bottlenecks and machine breakdowns and this may result in an increase in unit variable costs because of diminishing returns to scale (See 'Economist's model' in Chapter 9).

(c) The budget committee should consist of high level executives who represent the major segments of the business. For example, the committee might consist of the chief executive (or his or her deputy), the production manager, the marketing manager, the management accountant and the human resource manager. Its major task is to communicate the long-term objectives of the organization, ensure that the budgets are realistically established and that they are coordinated satisfactorily.

Reclamation Division Performance Report – 4 weeks to 31 May:
Original budget   250 tonnes
Actual output   200 tonnes

	Budget based on 200 tonnes	Actual	Variance	Comments
Controllable expenses:				
Wages and social security costs[a]	43 936	46 133	2197A	
Fuel[b]	15 000	15 500	500A	
Consumables[c]	2 000	2 100	100A	
Power[d]	1 500	1 590	90A	
Directly attributable overheads[e]	20 000	21 000	1000A	
	82 436	86 323	3887A	
Non-controllable expenses:				
Plant maintenance[e]	5 950	6 900	950A	
Central services[e]	6 850	7 300	450A	
	12 800	14 200	1400A	
Total	95 236	100 523	5287A	

Notes:
[a] 6 employees $\times$ 4 teams $\times$ 42 hours per week $\times$ £7.50 per hour $\times$ 4 weeks = £30 240
[b] 200 tonnes $\times$ £75
[c] 200 tonnes $\times$ £10
[d] £500 + (£5 $\times$ 200) = £1500
[e] It is assumed that directly attributable expenses, plant maintenance and central services are non-variable expenses.

Task 2
(a)   (i) Past knowledge can provide useful information on future outcomes but ideally budgets ought to be based on the most up-to-date information. Budgeting should be related to the current environment and the use of past information that is two years old can only be justified where the operating conditions and environment are expected to remain unchanged.
   (ii) For motivation and planning purposes budgets should represent targets based on what we are proposing to do. For control purposes budgets should be flexed based on what was actually done so that actual costs for actual output can be compared with budgeted costs for the actual output. This ensures that valid comparisons will be made.
   (iii) For variable expenses the original budget should be reduced in proportion to reduced output in order to reflect cost behaviour. Fixed costs are not adjusted since they are unaffected in the short-term by output changes. Flexible budgeting ensures that like is being compared with like so that reduced output does not increase the probability that favourable cost variances will be reported. However, if less was produced because of actual sales being less than budget this will result in an adverse sales variance and possibly an adverse profit variance.
   (iv) Plant maintenance costs are apportioned on the basis of capital values and therefore newer equipment (with higher written-down values) will be charged with a higher maintenance cost. Such an approach does not provide a meaningful estimate of maintenance resources consumed by departments since older equipment is likely to be more expensive to maintain. The method of recharging should be reviewed and ideally based on estimated usage according to maintenance records. The charging of the overspending by the maintenance department to user departments is questionable since

this masks inefficiencies. Ideally, maintenance department costs should be recharged based on actual usage at budgeted cost and the maintenance department made accountable for the adverse spending (price) variance.

(v) The comments do not explain the causes of the variances and are presented in a negative tone. No comments are made, nor is any praise given, for the favourable variances.

(vi) Not all variances should be investigated. The decision to investigate should depend on both their absolute and relative size and the likely benefits arising from an investigation.

(vii) Central service costs are not controllable by divisional managers. However, even though the divisional manager cannot control these costs there is an argument for including them as non-controllable costs in the performance report. The justification for this is that divisional managers are made aware of central service costs and may put pressure on central service staff to control such costs more effectively. It should be made clear to divisional managers that they are not accountable for any non-controllable expenses that are included in their performance reports.

Question 14.11

Task 1

(a)

	Quarter 1 units	Quarter 2 units	Quarter 3 units	Quarter 4 units
Actual sales volume	420 000	450 000	475 000	475 000
Seasonal variation	+25 000	+15 000	—	240 000
Deseasonalized sales volumes	395 000	435 000	475 000	515 000

(b) The trend is for sales volume to increase by 40 000 units each quarter:

Forecast for next year	Quarter 1 units	Quarter 2 units	Quarter 3 units	Quarter 4 units
Trend projection	555 000	595 000	635 000	675 000
Seasonal variation	+25 000	+15 000	—	−40 000
Forecast sales volumes	580 000	610 000	635 000	635 000

Task 2

(a) Seasonal variations represent consistent patterns in sales volume that occur throughout each year. For example, the seasonal variation of +25 000 for Quarter 1 indicates that sales volume in the first quarter tends to be 25 000 units higher than the underlying trend in sales. In contrast, the seasonal variation of −40 000 in Quarter 4 indicates that sales in this quarter tend to be 40 000 units lower than the underlying trend in sales.

To derive the deseasonalized data the seasonal variations must be removed so that a trend can be observed. The above figures indicate an increase of 40 000 units per quarter. This trend is concealed when the actual data is observed because of the distorting effects of seasonal variations. Observations of the actual data suggests that the rate of increase in sales is declining.

(b) Provided that the observed trend in deseasonalized data continues the deseasonalized data can be used to project the trend in future sales. The trend values are adjusted by seasonal variations in each quarter to predict actual sales.

Task 3

(a) A fixed budget is a budget for the planned level of activity and budgeted costs are not adjusted to the actual level of activity. A fixed budget is used at the planning stage because an activity level has to be initially determined so that all department activities can be coordinated to meet the planned level of activity. However, it is most unlikely that actual activity will be the same as the planned level of activity. For example, if the actual level of activity is greater than budgeted level of activity then those costs that vary with the level of activity will be greater than the budgeted costs purely because of changes in activity. It is clearly inappropriate for variable costs to compare actual costs at one level of activity with budgeted costs at another level of activity. The original fixed budget must be adjusted to reflect the budgeted expenditure at the actual level of activity. This procedure is called flexible budgeting. The resulting comparison of actual costs with a flexible budget is more meaningful for cost control because the effect of the change in the activity level has been eliminated.

(b) Possible activity indicators include number of deliveries made, miles travelled and journeys made.

(c) See 'Flexible budgets' in Chapter 14 for the answer to this question.

Task 4

(a) Production budget for product Q

	(units)
Forecast sales for year	18 135
Increase in stock (15% × 1200)	180
Finished units required	18 315
Quality control loss (1/99)	185
Total units input to production	18 500

(b) Direct labour budget for product Q

	(hours)
Active labour hours required (18 500 × 5)	92 500
Idle time allowance (7.5/92.5)	7 500
Total hours to be paid for	100 000
Standard hourly rate	£6
Budgeted labour cost	£600 000

(c) Material usage budget for material M

	(kg)
Material required for processing	
18 500 units (× 9 kg)	166 500
Wastage (10/90)	18 500
Material usage for year	185 000

(d) Material purchases budget for material M

	(kg)
Material required for production input	185 000
Increase in material stocks (12%)	960
Expected loss in stores	1 000
Material purchases required	186 960

Task 5

The implications of the shortage is that the budget plans cannot be achieved and the availability of material is the limiting factor. If the limiting factor cannot be removed the materials purchase budget should be the first budget to be prepared and all the other budgets coordinated to ensure the most efficient usage of materials. The following four possible actions could be taken to overcome the problem:

(i) Seek alternative supplies for material M. Possible problems include the reliability and quality of materials delivered by new suppliers. New suppliers should be carefully vetted prior to entering into any contracts or making company plans dependent on deliveries from new suppliers.

(ii) Reduce the budgeted sales of product Q. This will lead to loss in profits and the possible permanent loss of customers to competitors if the competitors are able to meet customer demand.

(iii) Reduce the stock levels for product Q and material M. The danger with this course of action is that stocks may not be available when required which could lead to disruptions in production and lost sales.

(iv) Reduce the wastage of material M and the defective output of product Q. This course of action will cause problems if quality standards are reduced resulting in inferior quality output. This could have a harmful effect on future sales. Problems will not be caused if quality standards are maintained and improved working practices result in a reduction of waste and defective output.

Question 14.12 *Task 1 (a)*

Calculation of unit variable costs

	Original budget	Revised budget	Difference	Variable unit cost[a]
Units	24 000	20 000	4 000	
Variable costs				
Material	216 000	180 000	£36 000	£9
Labour	288 000	240 000	£48 000	£12
Semi-variable costs				
Heat, light and power	31 000	27 000	£4 000	£1
Analysis of heat, light and power				
Variable cost	£24 000	£20 000		
Total cost	£31 000	£27 000		
Fixed cost	£7 000	£7 000		

Note
[a]Unit variable cost = change in total cost/change in volume

Task 1 (b)

Rivermede Ltd – flexible budget statement for the year ended 31 May

	Revised budget	Actual results		Variance
Production and sales (units)	22 000	22 000		
Variable costs	(£)	(£)		(£)
Material 22 000 × £9	198 000	214 320	(£206 800 + £7520)	6320 (A)
Labour 22 000 × £12	264 000	255 200		8800 (F)
Semi-variable cost				
Heat, light and power				
(22 000 × £1) + £7000	29 000	25 880	(£33 400 − £7520)	3120 (F)
Fixed costs				
Rent, rates and depreciation	40 000	38 000		2000 (F)
	531 000	533 400		2400 (A)

Task 2 (a)
The original statement compares the actual cost of producing 22 000 units with a budget for 20 000 units. This is not comparing like with like. The flexible budget shows what budgeted costs would have been for the actual production level of 22 000 units. Because actual production was greater than budgeted production of 20 000 units variable costs are likely to be higher and this comparison will result in

an adverse effect on variable cost variances. The fact that overall variances are smaller when comparisons are made with the flexible budget is due to flexing the budget and not to participative budgeting.

Task 2 (b)
The report should indicate that favourable variances may have arisen for the following reasons:
     (i) Controllable factors due to the more efficient usage of direct labour and heating, light and power.
    (ii) Budget participation may have resulted in the creation of slack through an overstatement of budgeted costs.
    (iii) Uncontrollable factors such as a reduction in the prices charged to Rivermede for rent and rates.

Task 2 (c)
The report should include the following items:
     (i) The increased sales may have been due to a general increase in demand rather than the effort of the salesforce.
    (ii) The original budget of 24 000 units may have been over-estimated or the revised budget of 20 000 units may have been understated due to the sales director creating slack by deliberately understating demand.

Question 14.13

Task 1 (a)
For 2001 x takes on a value of 9.
Therefore annual demand $(y) = 640 + (40 \times 9) = 1000$
weekly demand $= 1\,000/25 = 40$ holidays

Task 1 (b)
Weaknesses of the least squares regression formula include:
     (i) The formula assumes a linear relationship based on time but demand for holidays may not be a linear function of time.
    (ii) Seasonal variations are ignored. Demand may vary throughout the holiday season with some holiday weeks being more popular than others.
    (iii) It ignores changes in holidaymakers' tastes such as a change in demand from short haul to long haul or 10-day holidays to short-break holidays.
    (iv) Cyclical fluctuations are ignored. Demand for holidays is likely to vary depending on the state of the economy, such as boom or recession.

Task 2 (a)

Revised cost statement 10 days ended 27 November

Flexed budget	*Note*	*Budget* (£)	*Actual* (£)	*Variance* (£)
Aircraft seats	1	18 000	18 600	600 A
Coach hire		5 000	4 700	300 F
Hotel rooms	2	14 300	14 200	100 F
Meals	3	4 560	4 600	40 A
Tour guide		1 800	1 700	100 F
Advertising		2 000	1 800	200 F
		45 660	45 600	60 F

Notes
1   £450 × 40 because purchases are in blocks of 20 seats
2   £70 × 10 days × 34 tourists × 0.5   £11 900
     £60 × 10 days × 4 tourists   £2 400
                            £14 300

3   £12 × 10 days × 38 tourists

Task 2 (b)

The original budget is a fixed budget based on the anticipated demand when the budget was set. If actual demand is different from anticipated demand a fixed budget is inappropriate for control purposes because it does not ensure that like is compared with like. See the answer to Question 14.12 for an explanation of this point. The revised flexible budget shows what costs should have been for the volume of passengers taken on the holiday. This ensures that a more meaningful comparison of budget and actual costs is made.

Task 2 (c)

The following factors should be considered:
  (i)   the absolute amount of the variance;
  (ii) the relative amount of the variance expressed as a percentage of budgeted costs;
  (iii) the trend in variances by examining the cumulative variances for the period;
  (iv) whether or not the variance is controllable;
  (v)   the cost and benefits from investigating the variance.

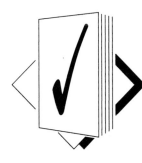

Standard costing and variance analysis

Solutions to Chapter 15 questions

Question 15.1   Labour efficiency variance   = [Standard hours – Actual hours (25 600)] × Standard rate (£7.50)

     = £8 250A

     = £7.50 × standard hours – (25 600 × £7.50) = – £8 250

£7.50 × standard hours   = £183 750

Standard hours   = 24 500

Answer = B

Question 15.3   Budgeted overhead rate = £10 per hour

Actual volume was 1000 standard hours less than budget thus causing an under-absorption of £10 000. Actual expenditure was £1400 more than budget thus resulting in an under-absorption of £1400.

Answer = C

Question 15.4

	(£)
Actual cost	16 380
Less adverse price variance	1 170
Actual purchases at standard price	15 210

Standard price = £15 210/7 800 kg = £1.95

Answer = A

Question 15.5

Sales volume variance = (Actual sales volume − Budgeted sales volume) × Standard profit margin
= (11 000 − £100 000/£8) £2.50 = £3750A

Sales price variance = (Actual price − Budgeted price) × Actual sales volume
= (£9 − £8) × 11 000 = £11 000F

Answer = A

Question 15.6

Efficiency variance = (Standard hours − Actual hours) Standard rate
= (4650 × 4 hrs = 18 600 − 19 100) £5.40
= £2700A

Rate variance = (Standard rate − Actual rate) Actual hours
= (£5.40 − £98 350/19 100) 19 100
= £4790F

Answer = E

Question 15.7

Efficiency variance = (Standard hours − Actual hours) × Standard rate
= (Standard hours × Standard rate) − (Actual hours − Standard rate)

− £36,000A = (5792 × 6.5 hrs × £5 = £188 240) − (AH × £5)
5AH = £188 240 + £36 000
AH = 44 848

Answer = D

Question 15.8

Sales margin price variance = (Actual margin – standard margin) × Actual volume
= [(£22 440/850 – £12) – £15] × 850 = £510A

Sales margin volume variance = (Actual volume – Budgeted volume) × Standard margin
= (850 – 800) × £15 = £750F

Answer = E

Question 15.9

Direct materials price variance = (Standard price – Actual price) × Actual quantity purchased
= (Standard price × Actual quantity purchased) – Actual cost
= (£0.40 × 8200) – £3444
= £164A

Direct materials usage variance = (Standard quantity – Actual quantity) × Standard price
= [(870 × 8kg) – 7150 kg] × £0.40
= £76 A

See the section in Chapter 15 headed 'Calculation of quantity purchased or quantity used' for an explanation of why it is preferable to calculate price variances on the basis of quantity purchased.

Answer = D

Wage rate variance	= (Standard rate – Actual rate) × Actual hours

Question 15.10

Wage rate variance
= (Standard rate – Actual rate) × Actual hours
= (Actual hours × Standard rate) – Actual cost
= (13 450 × £12 = £161 400) – £159 786
= £1614F

Labour efficiency variance = [Standard hours – Actual hours] × Standard rate
= (3350 × 4 hours = 13 400 – 13 450) × £12 = £600A

Answer = D

Question 15.12

Task
(a) Soap pack price variance = (Standard price – Actual price) Actual quantity
= (£1.20 – £1.30) 920 = £92A
= (£1.20 – £1.40) 1130 = £226A
                        £318A

Soap pack usage variance = (Standard quantity – Actual quantity) Standard price
= (8400 – 8580) £1.20
= £216A

Cleaning labour rate variance = (Standard rate – Actual rate) Actual hours
= (£3.60 – £3) 1850 = £1110F
= (£3.60 – £4.50) 700= £630A
                        £480F

Cleaning labour efficiency
variance = (Standard hours – Actual hours) Standard rate
= (8400 × 0.25 hours = 2100 – 2550) £3.60
= £1620A

(b) (i) The soap price variance could be due to inflation and a general increase in the market price. In such circumstances the standard price should be altered to reflect the current standard price.
(ii) The adverse soap usage variance could be due to theft or excess issues. Managers should check that stocks are securely locked away and that only the standard quantity is issued each day.
(iii) The labour rate variance may have arisen because proportionately less weekend work was undertaken than that allowed for in the standard. It may be appropriate to maintain separate standards for weekend and non-weekend work and separate records so that variances can be reported for both categories of labour.
(iv) The standard time may represent an inappropriate standard that must be changed. Alternatively, excessive idle time may have occurred because of rooms not being vacated when the cleaners are being paid. Working practices and vacation procedures should be investigated to ensure that vacation is synchronized with when the cleaners are employed for cleaning the rooms.

Question 15.13

Task 1
(a) Material price variance = (Standard price – Actual price) × Actual quantity
= (Standard price × Actual quantity) – Actual cost
= (78 000 × £20) – £1 599 000
= £1 560 000 – £1 599 000
= £39 000A

Material usage
variance = (Standard quantity − Actual quantity) × Standard price
= (9500 × 8 = 76 000 litres − 78 000 litres) × £20
= £40 000 Adverse

Wage rate variance = (Standard price − Actual price) × Actual hours
= (Standard price × Actual hours) − Actual cost
= (£6 × 39 000 = £234 000) − £249 600
= £15 600A

Labour efficiency variance = (Standard hours − Actual hours) × Standard rate
= (9500 × 4 = 38 000 − 39 000) × £6
= £6000A

(b)

		(£)	(£)
Standard cost of production (9500 × £184)			1 748 000
Add adverse variances:	Material price	39 000	
	Material usage	40 000	
	Wage rate	15 600	
	Labour efficiency	6 000	100 600
Actual cost			1 848 600

Task 2

(a) Material used in standard quantities
(1500 × 100/80 × 8 litres) = 15 000
Standard usage for special order (1500 × 8) = 12 000
Material usage variance arising from special order
(3000 kg × £20) = £60 000A
Material price variance arising from special order
(15 000 kg × (£22 − £20)) = £18 000A
Wage rate variance arising from special order
(1500 × 4 hrs × £6 × 50%) = £18 000A

(b) Revised standard price (247.2/240 × £20)   £20.60
Increase over original standard   £0.60
Material used excluding special order (78 000 − 15 000)   63 000 litres
Price variance arising from price increase (63 000 × £0.60)   £37 800A

(c)

	(£)	(£)
Standard cost of production		1 748 000
Add non-controllable variances		
Special order material usage variance	60 000A	
Special order material price variance	30 000A	
Special order wage rate variance	18 000A	
Material price variance due to increase in market price	37 800A	145 800A
Add controllable variances:		
Material price (£39 000 − £30 000 − £37 800)	28 800F	
Material usage (£40 000 − £60 000)	20 000F	
Wage rate (£15 600 − £18 000)	2 400F	
Labour efficiency	6 000A	45 200F
Actual cost		1 848 600

(d) The answer should draw attention to the fact that the divisional total variance was £100 600 but £145 800 was not controllable by the manager. This consisted of £37 800 arising from an increase in market prices and £108 000 arising from the special order. The manager should be congratulated on the favourable controllable variances.

If the index of material prices was applicable to the type of materials used by the division then the standard should be altered to reflect the price change. The profitability of the special order should be recalculated after taking into account the extra cost arising from the adverse variances and the sales director informed. The sales director should also be requested to provide details of special orders to the relevant managers so that steps can be taken to ensure that the materials can be obtained from the normal supplier.

Question 15.14

(a) £3 is the sum of the predicted unit costs given in the question.
Therefore budgeted profit = (£7.50 budgeted selling price – £3) × 750 budgeted menus sold = £3375.

(b) Actual profit = Actual sales (860 × £7) – Actual costs (£2548) = £3472

Note that the actual cost is the sum of the direct costs given in the question.

(c) The usage (quantity) cost variances for all of the ingredients can be calculated as follows:
((Actual sales quantity × standard quantity of ingredients per menu) × Actual quantity) × standard price

		(£)
Mushrooms ((860 × 0.1 kgs) – 90 kgs) × £3	=	12A
Beef ((860 × 0.1 kgs) – 70 kg) × £15	=	240F
Potatoes (860 × 0.2 kgs) × £0.25	=	2A
Vegetables (860 × 0.3 kgs) × £0.90	=	11A
Fresh fruit (860 × 0.15 kgs) × £3	=	33A

The price variance for all of the ingredients is:

(Standard price – Actual price) × Actual quantity of ingredients
= (Actual × standard price) – (Actual quantity × Actual price)

		£
Mushrooms (90 kgs × £3) – (£300)	=	30A
Beef (70 kgs × £15) – (£1148)	=	98A
Potatoes (180 kgs × £0.25) – (£40)	=	5F
Vegetables (270 kgs × £0.90) – (£250)	=	7A
Fresh fruit (140 kgs × £3) – (£450)	=	30A

Details of prices and quantities per menu are not given for cream and other ingredients so it is not possible to analyse the total variance by price and quantity. The total variance is calculated as follows:

(Actual sales quantity × standard price) – Actual cost

		£
Cream etc. (860 × £0.20) – £160	=	12A
Other ingredients (860 × £0.23) – £200	=	2A
Sales price variance	= (Actual selling price – Budgeted selling price) × Actual sales quantity	
	= (£7.0 – £7.50) × 860	= £430A
Sales volume variance	= (Actual volume – Budgeted volume) × Standard margin	
	= (860 – 750) × £4.50	= 495F

Reconciliation of budgeted and actual profit

			(£)
Budgeted profit			3375
Sales volume variance			495
Budgeted profit on actual sales			3870
Sales price variance			430
			3440

	Price	Usage	
Ingredients:	(£)	(£)	
Mushrooms	30A	12A	42A
Cream, etc.	n/a	n/a	12F
Beef	98A	240F	142F
Potatoes	5F	2A	3F
Vegetables	7A	11A	18A
Other	n/a	n/a	2A
Fresh fruit	30A	33A	63A
Actual profit			3472

(d) The sales volume and sales price are the two most significant variances. The adverse sales price variance is due to a reduction in selling price which may have been implemented to stimulate demand. The reduction in the selling price would appear to be the reason for the increase in sales volume and the favourable variance. Overall the selling price reduction has been beneficial with the favourable volume variance exceeding the adverse price variance.

Question 15.16 (a) It is assumed that the term 'standard costing profit statement' means budgeted profit statement (i.e. budgeted sales less standard cost of budgeted sales). Alternatively, the term 'standard costing profit statement' can be interpreted as actual sales less standard cost of actual sales. Adopting this interpretation will mean that a sales volume variance will not be reported.

Budgeted profit statement:

		(£)
Sales (16 000 units × £140)		2 240 000
Materials		
007 (16 000 × 6 kg × £12.25)	1 176 000	
XL90 (16 000 × 3 kg × £3.20)	153 600	
Labour		
16 000 × 4.5 hours × £8.40	604 800	
Overheads		
All fixed (given)	86 400	1 882 560
Profit		219 200

Actual profit statement:

		(£)
Sales (15 400 units × £138.25)		2 129 050
Materials		
007	1 256 640	
XL90	132 979	
Labour	612 766	
Overheads	96 840	2 099 225
Profit		29 825

Note that the above statements are prepared on a marginal costing basis.

(b) Material price variance   = (Standard price − Actual price) × Actual quantity
                              = (Actual quantity × Standard price) − Actual cost

Material 007   = (98 560 kg × £12.25) − £1 256 640 = £49 280A

Material XL90   = (42 350 kg × £3.20) − £132 979 = £2541F

Material usage variance = (Standard quantity − Actual quantity) × Standard price

Material 007   = (15 400 × 6 kg = 92 400 − 98 560) × £12.25 = £75 460

Material XL90   = (15 400 × 3 kg = 46 200 − 42 350) × £3.20 = £12 320F

Wage rate variance   = (Standard price − Actual price) × Actual hours
                              = (£8.40 − £8.65) × £612 766/£8.65 = £17 710A

Labour efficiency variance   = (Standard hours − Actual hours) × Standard price
                                = (15 400 × 4.5 hrs = 69 300 − 70 840[a]) × £8.40 = £12 936A

Fixed overhead expenditure = Budgeted cost − Actual cost
                                = £86 400 − £96 840 = £10 440A

Sales margin price   = (Actual price − Budgeted price) × Actual volume
                                = (£138.25 − £140) × 15 400 = £26 950A

Sales margin volume   = (Actual volume – Budgeted volume) × Standard margin
                                = (15 400 − 16 000) × £19.10[b] − £11 460A

Notes:

[a] Actual hours = £612 766/£8.65 = 70 840

	(£)
[b] Budgeted contribution margin = Selling price	140.00
Less Direct materials (6 × £12.25) + (3 × £3.20)	83.10
Direct labour (4.5 × £8.40)	37.80
	19.10

Reconciliation statement:	(£)
Budgeted profit	219 200
Add favourable variances (£2541 + £12 320)	14 861
	234 061
Less adverse variances (£49 280 + £75 460 + £17 710 + £12 936)	
(+ £10 440 + £26 950 + £11 460)	204 236
Actual profit	29 825

(c) The purchase of cheap, poor quality materials below standard price will result in a favourable price variance but may be the cause of an adverse material usage and labour efficiency variance. Similarly, the use of unskilled instead of skilled labour will result in a favourable wage rate variance and may be the cause of an adverse material usage variance arising from spoilt work and excessive usage of materials. The use of less skilled labour may also result in an adverse labour efficiency variance if the workers are not as efficient as skilled workers.

Question 15.21

(a) *Calculation of standard unit cost*

	(£)
Materials (336 000 kg/240 000 units = 1.40 kg at £4.10 per kg)	5.74
Direct labour (216 000 hrs/240 000 units = 0.9 hrs at £4.50 per hour)	4.05
Variable overhead (0.9 hrs at £475 200/216 000 hrs = £2.20 per hour)	1.98
Fixed overhead (£1 521 600/240 000 units)	6.34
	18.11

Variance calculations

Material price: (Standard price − Actual price) × Actual quantity
                (£4.10 − £1 245 980/313 060 kg) × 313 060 kg   £37 566F

Material usage: (Standard quantity − Actual quantity) × Standard price
(220 000 units × 1.40 kg = 308 000 kg − 313 060 kg)
× £4.10   £20 746A

Wage rate: (Standard rate − Actual rate) × Actual hours
(£4.50 − £886 886/194 920 hrs) × 194 920 hrs   £9 746A

Labour efficiency: (Standard hours − Actual hours) × Standard rate
(220 000 units × 0.9 hrs)
= 198 000 hours − 194 920 hrs × £4.50   £13 860F

Variable overhead efficiency: (Standard hours − Actual hours)
× Standard rate
(198 000 − 194 920) × £2.20   £6 776F

Variable overhead expenditure: (Actual hours × Standard rate) −
Actual cost
(194 920 × £2.20 = £428 824) −
£433 700   £4 876A

Fixed overhead expenditure: (Budgeted cost − Actual cost)
(£1 521 600 − £1 501 240)   £20 360F

Fixed overhead volume: (Actual output − Budget output) ×
Standard rate
(220 000 − 240 000) × £6.34   £126 800A

Total variances   £831 606A

(b) The favourable labour efficiency variance may be due to:
  (i) Efficient production in less than standard time due to efficiency of the labour force.
  (ii) Easily attainable standard.
  (iii) Lack of production delays.
    The variable overheads are absorbed on the basis of direct labour hours and therefore the variable overhead efficiency variance will be a direct result of the labour efficiency variance.
    The fixed overhead volume variance is due to actual production being less than budgeted production. This may be due to reduced sales or reduction in stock levels. However, because the fixed overhead is a sunk cost changes in volume will not result in a change in fixed overheads incurred and the variance is of a dubious value for cost control purposes.

Question 15.22 (a) Because some variable overheads vary with machine hours and other variable overheads vary with direct labour hours separate variable overhead efficiency and expenditure variances should be computed for machine-related and labour-related variable overheads.

Variable overhead efficiency variance:
  (Standard hours − Actual hours) × Standard rate
Machine related = (5450 × 4 hours = 21 800 − 22 000) × £8 = £1600A
Labour related = (5450 × 2 hours = 10 900 − 10 800) × £4 = £400F

Variable overhead expenditure variance:
  (Actual hours × Standard rate) − Actual variable overheads incurred
Machine related = 22 000 × £8 = £176 000 − £176 000 = Nil
Labour related = 10 800 × £4 = £43 200 − £42 000 = £1200F

Fixed overhead expenditure variance
$$= \text{Budgeted cost} - \text{Actual cost}$$
$$= 5500 \text{ units} \times £20 = £110\,000 - £109\,000$$
$$= £1000F$$

Fixed overhead volume $= (\text{Actual production} - \text{Budgeted production}) \times$ Standard rate
$$= (5450 - 5500) \times £20 = £1000A$$

(b) The variable overhead machine-related efficiency variance arises because machine hours exceeded target (standard) hours that should have been used for the actual output. Because it is assumed that some variable overheads vary with machine hours the excess usage has resulted in additional spending on variable overheads. Failure to maintain machinery may have resulted in the use of hours in excess of standard.

The variable overhead labour-related variance arises because actual direct labour hours were less than the hours that should have been used for the actual output. This has resulted in reduced expenditure on those variable overheads that vary with direct labour hours. An improvement in the efficiency of direct labour has resulted in the favourable variance.

The variable overhead labour-related expenditure variance arises because actual spending was less than budgeted spending flexed to the actual level of activity. Prices paid for variable overhead items (e.g. indirect materials) may have been lower than the figures used to derive the budgeted expenditure. For a more detailed answer see the section on variable overhead expenditure variance in Chapter 15.

(c) See the comparison of ABC and traditional product costing systems in Chapter 11 for the answer to this question. In particular, the answer should demonstrate how the use of multiple cost drivers should result in the reporting of more accurate product costs than when a single cost driver is used. In order to understand and manage costs more effectively there is a need to measure overhead resource consumption using cost drivers that are the causes of overhead expenditure. Different cost drivers, rather than a single cost driver, provide a better explanation of cost behaviour. Thus multiple cost drivers should also result in better cost management (see the section on activity-cost management in Chapter 14 for a more detailed explanation of this point).

(a) *Standard cost of output produced (18 000 units)*   **Question 15.23**

	(£)
Direct materials	864 000
Direct labour	630 000
Variable production overhead	180 000
Fixed production overhead	900 000
	2 574 000

(b)	Standard cost of output (£)	Variances (£)	Actual cost (£)
Direct materials	864 000		
Price variance^a		76 000 (F)	
Usage variance^b		48 000 (A)	
Actual cost			836 000
Direct labour	630 000		
Rate variance^c		16 800 (A)	
Efficiency variance^d		42 000 (F)	
Actual cost			604 800
Variable production overhead	180 000		
Expenditure variance^e		4 000 (A)	
Efficiency variance^f		12 000 (F)	
Actual cost			172 000
Fixed production overhead	900 000		
Expenditure variance^g		30 000 (A)	
Volume variance^h		100 000 (A)	
Actual cost			1 030 000
	2 574 000	68 800 (A)	2 642 800

Notes
^{a} (Standard price − Actual price) × Actual quantity
  (£12 − £836 000/76 000) × 76 000 = £76 000 (F)
^{b} (Standard quantity − Actual quantity) × Standard price
  (18 000 × 4 kg = 72 000 − 76 000) × £12 = £48 000 (A)
^{c} (Standard rate − Actual rate) × Actual hours
  (£7 − £604 800/84 000) × 84 000 = £16 800 (A)
^{d} (Standard hours − Actual hours) × Standard rate
  (18 000 × 5 hrs = 90 000 − 84 000) × £7 = £42 000 (F)
^{e} (Actual hours × Standard rate) − Actual cost
  (84 000 × £2 = £168 000 − £172 000 = £4000 (A)
^{f} (Standard hours − Actual hours) × Standard rate
  (18 000 × 5 hrs = 90 000 − 84 000) × £2 = £12 000 (F)
^{g} Budgeted fixed overheads − Actual fixed overheads
  (20 000 × £50 = £1 000 000 − £1 030 000) = £30 000 (A)
^{h} (Actual output − Budgeted output) × Standard rate
  (18 000 − 20 000) × £50 = £100 000 (A)

(c) The statement in (b) can be used to provide a detailed explanation as to why actual cost exceeded standard cost by £68 800 for the output achieved. The statement provides attention-directing information by highlighting those areas that require further investigation. Thus management can concentrate their scarce time on focusing on those areas that are not proceeding according to plan. By investigating variances, management can pinpoint inefficiencies and take steps to avoid them re-occurring. Alternatively, the investigation may indicate that the current standards are inappropriate and need changing to take account of the changed circumstances. This may result in an alteration in the plans or more up-to-date information for decision-making.

(a)   (i) Material price variance $= (SP - AP)AQ = (SP \times AQ) - (AQ \times AP)$ **Question 15.24**

$= (£1.20 \times 142\,000) - £171\,820$

$= £1420A$

  (ii) Material usage variance $= (SQ - AQ)SP$

$= (1790 \times 9 = 16\,110 - 16\,270) \times £1.20$

$= £192A$

  (iii) Actual price per kg in period 1 = £1.21 (£171 820/142 000 kg)
The actual price per kg for period 2 is not given and must be calculated from the data given in the question.

Standard price = £1.20 × 1.06 = £1.272
$(SP \times AQ)$ = £1.272 × 147 400 (AQ) = £187 492.80
Price variance (£1031.80F)= $(SP \times AQ) - (AQ \times AP)$
             £1031.80F = £187 492.80 − (147 400 × AP)

$$AP = \frac{£187\,492.80 - £1031.80}{147\,400}$$

            = £1.265 per kg
Cost inflation   = (£1.265/£1.21 − 1) × 100% = 4.5%

  (iv) Actual usage per unit in period 1 = 16 270 kg/1790 units = 9.0894 kg
Actual usage in period 2 = 0.995 × 9 kg Standard usage = 8.995 kg
Change in usage (9.0894 − 8.995)/9.0894 × 100% = 1.5% improvement.

(b) See 'Types of cost standards' in Chapter 15 for the answer to this question.

(a)   (i) A fixed overhead volume variance only occurs with an absorption costing   **Question 15.26**
system. The question indicates that a volume variance has been reported. Therefore the company must operate an absorption costing system and report the sales volume variance in terms of profit margins, rather than contribution margins.

Budgeted profit margin = Budgeted profit (£4250)/Budgeted volume
                (1500 units)
                = £2.83

Adverse sales volume variance in units = £850/£2.83 = 300 units
Therefore actual sales volume was 300 units below budgeted sales volume
Actual sales volume = 1200 units (1500 units − 300 units)

  (ii) Standard quantity of material used per units of output:
    Budgeted usage (750 kg)/Budgeted production (1500 units) = 0.5 kg
Standard price = Budgeted material cost (£4500)/Budgeted usage
             (750 kg) = £6
Material usage variance = (Standard quantity − Actual Quantity) Standard
                    price
      £150A   = (1550 × 0.5 kg = 775 kg − AQ)£6
     − £150   = 4650 − 6AQ
      6AQ   = 4800
Actual quantity used   = 800 kg

  (iii) Material price variance = (Standard price − Actual price) × Actual
                       purchases
      £1000F   = (£6 − Actual price) × 1000 kg
      £1000F   = £6000 − 1000AP
      1000AP   = £5000
      AP   = £5 per kg
Actual material cost   = 1000 kg × £5 = £5000

(iv) Standard hours per unit of output = $\dfrac{\text{Budgeted hours (1125)}}{\text{Budgeted output (1500 units)}}$

= 0.75 hours

Standard wage rate = Budgeted labour cost (£4500)/Budgeted hours (1125)

= £4

Labour efficiency variance	= (Standard hours − Actual hours) × Standard rate
£150A	= (1550 × 0.75 = 1162.5 − Actual hours) × £4
− £150	= £4650 − 4AH
4AH	= £4800
Actual hours	= 1200

(v)

Total labour variance	= Standard cost − Actual cost
(£200A + £150A)	= (1550 × 0.75 hrs × £4) − Actual cost
£350A	= £4650 − Actual cost
Actual cost	= £5000

(vi) Standard variable overhead cost per unit

= $\dfrac{\text{Budgeted variable overheads (2250)}}{\text{Budgeted output (1500 units)}}$

= £1.50

Total variable overhead variance	= Standard cost − Actual cost
(£600A + £75A)	= (1550 × £1.50 = £2325) − Actual cost
£675A	= £2325 − Actual cost
Actual cost	= £3000

(vii)

Fixed overhead expenditure variance	= Budgeted cost − Actual cost
£2500F	= £4500 − Actual cost
Actual cost	= £2000

(b) See Chapter 15 for an explanation of the causes of the direct material usage, direct labour rate and sales volume variances.

Question 15.27 (a)

Wage rate variance	= (SP − AP)AH = (SP × AH) − (AP × AH)
	= (£5 × 53 workers × 13 weeks × 40 hrs) − £138 500
	= £700A
Labour efficiency	= (SH − AH)SP
SH (Standard hours)	= (35 000 × 0.4 hrs) + (25 000 × 0.56 hrs)
	= 28 000
AH (Actual hours)	= 53 workers × 13 weeks × 40 hrs = 27 560
Variance	= (28 000 − 27 560) × £5 = £2200A

(b)

Material price variance	= (SP − AP)AQ
	= (AQ × SP) − (AQ × AP)
£430F (given)	= 47 000 SP − £85 110
SP (Standard price)	= $\dfrac{£430 + 85\,110}{47\,000}$
	= £1.82

Material usage variance	= (SQ − AQ)SP
	= (SQ × SP) − (AQ × SP)
£320.32A (given)	= £1.82 SQ − (33 426 × £1.82)
− £320.32A	= £1.82SQ − £60 835.32
£1.82 SQ	= £60 515
SQ	= £60 515/£1.82 = 33 250
Note that SQ	= Actual production (35 000 units) × Standard usage
Therefore 35 000 × Standard usage = 33 250	
Standard usage	= 33 250/35 000
	= 0.95 kg per unit of component X

(c) For the answer to this question you should refer to the detailed illustration of the budget process shown in Chapter 13. In particular, the answer should indicate that if sales are the limiting factor the production budget should be linked to the sales budget. Once the production budget has been established for the two components, the production quantity of each component multiplied by the standard usage of material A per unit of component output determines the required quantity of material to meet the production requirements. The budgeted purchase quantity of material A consists of the quantity to meet the production usage requirements plus or minus an adjustment to take account of any planned change in the level of raw material stock.

Question 15.28

(a) (i) *Sales margin volume variance (Marginal costing):*
      (Actual volume − Budgeted volume) × Standard contribution margin per unit
      (9500 − 10 000) × Standard margin (SM) = £7500A
      500 SM = 7500
      Standard margin = £15

    (ii) *Sales margin volume variance (Absorption costing):*
      (Actual volume − Budgeted volume) × Standard profit margin per unit
      (9500 − 10 000) × Standard margin (SM) = £4500A
      500 SM = £4500
      Standard profit margin per unit = £9

   (iii) *Fixed overhead volume variance:*
      (Actual production − Budgeted production) × Standard rate
      (9700 − 10 000) × Standard rate = £1800A
      Standard fixed overhead rate per unit = £6
      Budgeted fixed overheads = 10 000 units × £6 = £60 000
      Fixed overhead expenditure variance   = £2500F
      Actual fixed overheads (£60 000 − £2500)   = £57 500

(b) Absorption costing unitizes fixed overheads and treats them as product costs whereas marginal costing does not charge fixed overheads to products. Instead, the total amount of fixed overheads is charged as an expense (period cost) for the period. A fixed overhead volume variance only occurs with an absorption costing system. Because marginal costing does not unitize fixed costs product margins are expressed as contribution margins whereas absorption costing expresses margins as profit margins. For a more detailed answer you should refer to the section on standard absorption costing in Chapter 15.

(c) See the section on volume variance in Chapter 15 for the answer to this question.

(d) See an illustration of ABC and traditional product costing systems in Chapter 11 and the section on activity-based cost management in Chapter 14 for the answer to this question.

Question 15.30

(a) *Workings*
    (i) *Material price variance identified on purchase of material*
      Variance = (SP − AP) × quantity purchased
      4 November (£1.04 − £10 530/10 000) × 10 000   = £130A
      23 November: (£1.04 − £8480/8000) × 8000   = £160A

Material Z stock account

	(£)		(£)
Opening balance		2/11 WIP (2000 × £1.04)	2 080
(9000 kg at £1.04)	9 360	7/11 WIP (4500 × £1.04)	4 680
4/11 Purchases			
(10 000 × £1.04)	10 400	20/11 WIP (4000 × £1.04)	4 160
23/11 Purchases			
(8000 × £1.04)	8 320	27/11 WIP (6000 × £1.04)	6 240
		Closing balance	
		(10 500 × £1.04)	10 920
	28 080		28 080

Creditors account

	4/11 Material Z stock	
	account	10 400
	4/11 Material price	
	variance account	130
	23/11 Material Z stock	
	account	8 320
	23/11 Material price	
	variance account	160

Material price variance account

4/11 Creditors account	130	30/11 Profit and Loss	
23/11 Creditors account	160	account	290

(ii) *Material price variance identified at time of issue of material*
Using the weighted average basis, the actual issue prices are calculated as follows:

	(£)
Opening balance (9000 × £1.07)	9 630
2 November issue (2000 × £1.07)	(2 140)
Balance 7000 at £1.07 (£7490/7000)	7 490
4 November purchase (10 000 kg)	10 530
Balance (17 000 kg at £1.06)	18 020
7 November issue (4500 × £1.06)	(4 770)
20 November issue (4000 × £1.06)	(4 240)
Balance (8500 × £1.06)	9 010
23 November purchase (8000 kg)	8 480
Balance (16 500 kg at £1.06)	17 490
27 November issue (6000 kg × £1.06)	6 360

Variance = (SP − AP) × actual issues
2 November: (£1.04 − £1.07) × 2000 = £60A
7 November: (£1.04 − £1.06) × 4500 = £90A
20 November: (£1.04 − £1.06) × 4000 = £80A
27 November: (£1.04 − £1.06) × 6000 = £120A

Note that the entries in the stock account in (a) (i) are based on the approach described in Chapter 15 whereby the stock account is debited at the standard cost and the variances are extracted at the time of purchase. Where variances are extracted at the time of issue, it is preferable to use an alternative approach when preparing the stock account. With this approach, the stock account is debited at actual cost, and issues are recorded at standard cost and the price variances are recorded within the stock account.

(iii)

Material Z

	(kg)	(£/unit)	(£)		(kg)	(£/unit)	(£)
1/11 Opening balance	9 000	1.07	9 630	2/11 Work-in-process	2 000	1.04	2 080
4/11 Purchases	10 000	1.053	10 530	2/11 Materials price variance			60
23/11 Purchases	8 000	1.06	8 480	7/11 Work-in-process	4 500	1.04	4 680
				7/11 Materials price variance			90
				20/11 Work-in-process	4 000	1.04	4 160
				20/11 Materials price variance			80
				27/11 Work-in-process	6 000	1.04	6 240
				27/11 Materials price variance			120
				30/11 Closing balance	10 500	1.06	11 130
	27 000		28 640		27 000		28 640

Material price variance

	(£)		(£)
2/11 Material Z	60	30/11 Profit and loss	350
7/11 Material Z	90		
20/11 Material Z	80		
27/11 Material Z	120		
	350		350

(b) The method by which variances are extracted at the time of purchase is preferred because variances are reported at the earliest opportunity. In addition, the stock recording system is simplified.

(c) *Workings*:

Equivalent units

	Materials	Labour and overhead
Completed production	9 970	9 970
Add closing WIP	8 000	6 000
	17 970	15 970
Less opening WIP	6 000	3 000
Equivalent production	11 970	12 970

Material usage variance
(actual usage − standard usage) × standard price
[6000 kg − (11 970 units × 0.5)] × £1.04
£15. 60A

Labour efficiency variance
(actual hours − standard hours) × standard rate
[1340 hrs − (12 970 units × 0.1)] × £4.80
£206.40A

Overhead variance
actual cost − standard cost
6680 − (12 970 units × 0.1 × £5.00)
£195A

Standard cost per unit: product X

Materials   0.5 kg × £1.04/kg   = £0.52
Direct labour 0.1 hrs × £4.80/hr   = £0.48
Overhead   0.1 hrs × £5.00/hr   = £0.50
                                        ——————
                                        £1.50

Process 1

	(£)		(£)
Opening balance:		Finished goods:	
Materials:		9970 units × £1.50	14 955
6000 units × £0.52		Closing balance:	
Direct labour and overhead:		Materials:	
3000 units × £0.98	6 060	8000 units × £0.52	
Materials:		Direct labour and overhead:	
6000 kilos × £1.04	6 240	6000 units × £0.98	10 040
Direct labour:		Material usage variance	15.6
1340 hours × £4.80	6 432	Labour efficiency variance	206.4
Overheads	6 680	Overhead variance	195
	25 412		25 412

Question 15.31 (a) *Variance analysis*

Material price = (standard price − actual price) × actual purchases
X   = (£20 − £20.50) × 9000
           = £4500A
Y   = (£6 − £5.50) × 5000
           = £2500F

Material usage = (standard usage − actual usage) × standard price
X   = (800 × 10 kg − 7800 kg) × £20
           = £4000F
Y   = (800 × 5 litres − 4300 litres) × £6
           = £1800A

Wage rate = [standard rate (£6) − actual rate (£24 150/4200)]
            × actual hours (4200)
          = £1050F

Labour efficiency = [standard hours (800 × 5 hrs) − actual hours (4200)]
                    × standard rate (£6)
                  = £1200A

Fixed overhead expenditure = budgeted cost (10 800/12 × £50)
                             − actual cost (£47 000)
                           = £2000A

Volume efficiency = [standard hours (800 × 5 hrs) − actual hours (4200)]
                    × (£50/5 hours)
                  = £2000A

Volume capacity[a] = [actual hours (4200) − budgeted hours[b] (4500)]
                     × FOAR (£50/5 hours)
                   = £3000A

Notes

[a] Note that the CIMA Terminology (at the time of setting the examination) described the volume variance as being equivalent to the volume capacity variance.

[b] Budgeted hours = monthly budgeted output (10 800/12) × 5 hrs

(b)

Stores control

	(£)		(£)
K Ltd: X (AQ × SP)	180 000	WIP: (SQ × SP)	160 000
C Ltd: Y (AQ × SP)	30 000	WIP: (SQ × SP)	24 000
Material usage variance (X)	4 000	Material usage variance (Y)	1 800
		Balance	28 200
	£214 000		£214 000

Wages control account

	(£)		(£)
Cash	20 150	Wages owing b/fwd	6 000
PAYE and NI	5 000	Labour efficiency	1 200
Accrued wages	5 000	WIP (SQ × SP)	24 000
Wage rate variance	1 050		
	£31 200		£31 200

WIP control account

	(£)		(£)
Stores control: X	160 000	Finished goods control a/c	248 000
Y	24 000		
Wages control	24 000		
Fixed overhead	40 000		
	£248 000		£248 000

Fixed overhead control

	(£)		(£)
Expense creditors	33 000	WIP (SQ × SP)	40 000
Depreciation provision	14 000	Expenditure variance	2 000
		Efficiency variance	2 000
		Capacity variance	3 000
	£47 000		£47 000

Finished goods control

	(£)		(£)
WIP control	£248 000	Cost of sales	£248 000

Cost of sales

	(£)		(£)
Finished goods control	£248 000	Profit and loss (P/L)	£248 000

Material price variance

	(£)		(£)
K Ltd: X	4500	C Ltd: Y	2500
		P/L	2000
	£4500		£4500

Material usage variance

	(£)		(£)
Stores control: Y	1800	Stores control: X	4000
P/L	2200		
	£4000		£4000

Labour rate variance

	(£)		(£)
P/L	£1050	Wages control	£1050

Labour efficiency variance

	(£)		(£)
Wages control	1200	P/L	1200

Fixed overhead expenditure variance

	(£)		(£)
Overhead control	2000	P/L	2000

Fixed overhead efficiency variance

	(£)		(£)
Overhead control	2000	P/L	2000

Fixed overhead capacity variance

	(£)		(£)
Overhead control	£3000	P/L	£3000

Sales

	(£)		(£)
P/L	320 000	Debtors	320 000

K Limited

			(£)
		Stores control	180 000
		Price variance account	4 500

C plc

	(£)		(£)
Price variance account	2500	Stores control	30 000

Expense creditors

			(£)
		Fixed overhead control	33 000

Provision for depreciation

		(£)
	Fixed overhead control	14 000

Profit and loss account

	(£)	(£)	(£)
Sales			320 000
Cost of sales			248 000
			72 000
Variances	(F)	(A)	
Material price	—	2 000	
usage	2200	—	
Labour rate	1050	—	
efficiency	—	1 200	
Overhead expenditure	—	2 000	
efficiency	—	2 000	
volume	—	3 000	
	3250	10 200	6 950
Gross profit			65 050

(c) The difference of £250 in the accounts is due to the fact that the material price variance has been calculated on purchases (instead of usage) and written off as a period cost. In the question the raw material stocks are recorded at actual cost, and therefore the £250 is included in the stock valuation and will be recorded as an expense next period.